Discarded
from the
Library

C LIBRARY

1550 0

D1028521

LEATHERCRAFTED

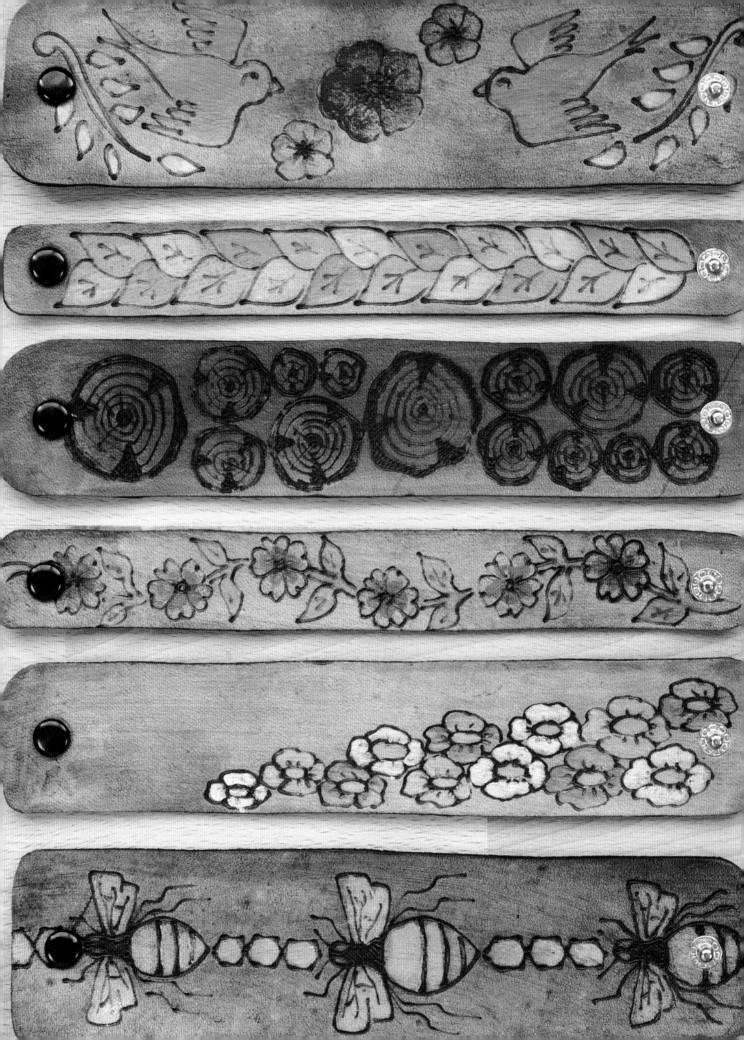

LeatherCrafted

A Simple Guide to Creating Unconventional Leather Goods

Orangeville Public Library
1 Mill Street
Orangeville, ON L9W 2M2

(519) 941-0610

Caitlin McNamara Sullivan
of Moxie & Oliver

Fons&Porter
CINCINNATI, OHIO

Contents

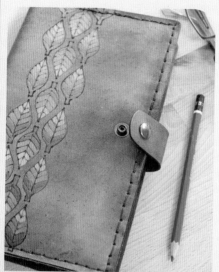

Introduction

My adventure and love affair with leathercraft started in 2004. I wasn't looking for a hobby, a career or a calling. I was simply looking for a new belt. At the time, I was working at a law firm as a paralegal and had every intention of going to law school. What turned my attention to leathercraft was my search for a belt that was interesting, something with pattern, that could spice up my professional attire and would not fall apart after a few months or years of use. When I couldn't find anything that met these criteria, I decided to make my own.

Bringing home my first belt blank along with some paint and dye, I had no idea what I was doing. As a child I had done some traditional leather "tooling" at family reunions, but it was limited to stamping pictures of bunnies and flowers on hair clips. Nothing complicated, and certainly nothing like what I wanted to do to this belt. With limited knowledge of leathercraft and a small budget, I began experimenting with ways to add pattern to that first strip of leather. I tried engraving it with a Dremel tool, carving it with my woodcutting tools and craft knives, burning it with a craft-store branding iron, painting it, dyeing it and sanding it. The end result was a belt covered in dogwood flowers and leaves in my favorite colors, resembling a carved piece of wood, and made of a single piece of leather. That first belt is still in use and holding up stunningly ten years later. I made the belt that I was searching for.

That year I used every technique I could think of to make belts for my husband and family for Christmas. In the next few years I began to experiment further. I bought hides and started making bags, pouches and wallets. I started a business and have refined my techniques over the years, and my husband often tells me that my work has "come so far" since I first started. But because I am self-taught, none of these techniques are so refined that you cannot learn them in an afternoon, with the right instruction.

I wrote this book so that, even if you have never worked with leather before, you can make yourself a beautiful and useful leather accessory in an afternoon. If you have worked with leather, this book will give you a tutorial on my unconventional leatherwork techniques. I will give you a short history of popular leathercraft before we get started, so when someone walks up to you and says, "Oh, you work with leather? My grandfather used to work with leather too," it will conjure up an image of what she is referring to. We will then go through the tools and materials you will use, practice some techniques and then get started on our projects. I have compiled ten of my favorite and most popular projects in this book so you can make yourself or someone else something beautiful, durable and unique out of leather.

I am providing you with the basics on my leatherworking techniques, and the rest is up to you! Where you go next with your craft may be driven by necessity. Do you need a wallet with more pockets? A bag in a different shape? You have the opportunity to make each piece a work of art, and there is no limit to what you can create.

A Brief History of Leather Crafting

Leather as a material is a mainstay in our daily wardrobe—shoes, wallets, belts, handbags and so on—but the art and craft of manipulating this material has fallen by the wayside over the last 250 years. Leather can be carved, painted, tooled, dyed, branded, embroidered, hammered, nailed/riveted, stitched and hardened, and the ability to manipulate it in so many ways makes it a truly distinctive medium. We have been using hides to create leather, and leather to create goods, since the earliest recorded human history. But without continued interest in the unique properties of leather, specifically vegetable-tanned leather, it will soon become no different from a fabric, used only to be cut and sewn, rather than shaped and embellished, and appreciated in its own right.

LEATHER TANNING

Our earliest ancestors recognized both the usefulness and the value of leather. Dating as far back as 20,000 B.C. in cave pictographs we see people wearing hides for warmth. Like every other part of the hunted animal, the hide was put to use. These early humans soon discovered that when an untreated animal hide was exposed to the elements, the hide would either rot or harden, depending on the climate they were in. It is unknown whether the hides in the first pictographs were preserved in any way, as there is no evidence of tanning in these early records.

We start to see the first instances of tanning around 8000 B.C. Early leather tanners would scrape the hair off of the hide with a sharpened stone and then treat the hide with animal brains or urine, which preserved the hide and kept it soft so it would neither rot nor dry out. These early tanners were in fact making heirloom-quality pieces; we have leather artifacts that date from 4000 B.C., and the oldest shoe found dates to shortly after, around 3500 B.C.

The earliest tanneries were comprised of vats where the leather was soaked in different substances to "tan" it. The tanning process of each civilization was slightly different, and a variety of substances was used in tanning processes worldwide: animal brains, dung from dogs and pigeons, urine, salt, alkaline lime and fat. Tanners would often employ children as dung gatherers, and human urine was collected to be used in the tanning process. In Pompeii, an ancient Roman town covered by Vesuvius in A.D. 79, there were public urinals to gather urine that was sold as an ingredient to be used both in tanning and as ammonia to bleach woolen togas. The excavated ruins of Pompeii also contain one of the oldest tanneries in the world.

During the early years of tanning, advances in methodology were few, and it isn't until 2000 B.C. that we start to see bark tanning, or what we today call "vegetable tanning." This process uses the tannins in tree bark to preserve the leather, and the process that we use today is predominantly the same as it was when first invented; we just use a larger variety of trees to obtain the bark. The process was slow; tanning a hide using the vegetable tanning process takes upwards of a month from start to finish and requires agitating the hide and moving it from one tanning vat to another periodically.

RISE OF GUILDS

Despite the overwhelming stenches coming from the tanneries, the specifics of tanning in its beginnings were guarded in secrecy, passed down through generations. As civilizations grew, especially in Europe, guilds developed to organize craftspeople and protect trade secrets.

In the Middle Ages, tanning, shoemaking, lace making, bag making and leather dyeing were all designated as separate crafts. Eventually saddlery and upholstery were added as guilds as well. The guilds served to regulate laws surrounding the artists and craftspeople, to protect them from competition from outsiders and to guarantee the quality of work. They functioned much like modern-day unions.

During the Middle Ages, leather crafters would add decorations, tooling and embellishments to their pieces. Leather tooling, a method where a tool or stamp is pressed (or hit with a mallet) into the leather to create a relief pattern, was also used. The Moors created beautifully tooled leather saddles, and in 1520 Spanish conquistador Hernando Cortés brought some of these saddles into the New World. The complex beauty of the tooled saddles was admired by those in the New World, and the style caught on in the southern region of North America as well as Central and South America. The Moorish leather tooling style is still present in the Southwest, Mexico, and Central and South America.

Shortly after the New World was first exposed to this beautifully tooled leather, other leather crafts made their way to the colonies. The first shoemakers (cordwainers) came in 1610 and in 1623, Experience Miller set up the first tannery in Plymouth, Massachusetts. This first tannery used vegetable tanning, and each hide took six months to transition from skin to a usable piece of leather. The guilds did not make the trip to the New World, however. The early colonies used apprentices who swore to keep the secrets of the masters but were not regulated or controlled by guilds.

THE INDUSTRIAL REVOLUTION AND NEW TECHNIQUES

Leather was widely used by crafts and tradespeople in the early colonies. The shoemaking business in particular was healthy and flourishing. Leather was also being used to make harnesses and saddles, books, upholstery, gloves, holsters, cartridge boxes, bellows, breeches and even coaches. The need for some of these objects, and the need for craftspeople to make them, changed dramatically with the Industrial Revolution. While there were some advances that were helpful to leathercraft, such as the 1809 invention of a mechanized hide splitter that could split hundreds of hides a day as opposed to the three or four that could be done manually, it was the beginning of the decline of leather crafting. By the mid-1800s the Industrial Revolution had taken hold and manufactured goods became easily accessible and more desirable than handcrafted pieces.

Mass production led to mass ownership, and purchasing power was equated with democracy. The quality of goods fell substantially during the Industrial Revolution, but the quantity of goods produced went up. Lower priced, machine-made goods replaced the beautiful handcrafted items of the pre-Industrial Revolution era. Craftspeople who were previously able to make a living at their craft were forced into factory jobs and struggled to survive. Those who had once worked in shoemaking turned their attention to shoe repairs, but as goods

became more and more disposable, even shoe repairs declined.

The late 1800s also saw an increase in travel by rail, which would be followed in quick succession by the invention of the automobile. The transition away from travel by horse and carriage changed the variety of leather goods that were needed. As people began to travel by rail or car, saddles, harnesses and carriages were no longer in high demand. Instead, people began to need luggage to take with them as they embarked on their rail travel. In 1897 Thierry Hermès, a former saddlemaker, began to make handbags and luggage for rail travel.

In the 1840s some in the medical community had begun to use sutures soaked in chromium, and by the nineteenth century this technique was adopted into the tanning community. Chromium tanning shortened the tanning process from several months to something that could be completed in a day, and when Robert Foes discovered he could improve the hide elasticity by a technique called "fatliquoring," chromium (or "chrome") tanning became another nail in the coffin of traditional leatherworking. Chromium tanned leather faster than vegetable/tree matter did, and it yielded a softer and suppler leather. The tanning process with chromium, however, was toxic both in process and waste.

Chromium tanning quickly and fiercely took over the leather tanning community. This new form of leather behaved more like a fabric than a stiff hide, and so lent itself easily to sewing and factory-style production. The quick turnaround from raw hide to leather was also an advantage with the pace of modern society. The chromium-tanned leather lacked many of the properties of the vegetable-tanned and earlier leathers, though: It could not be tooled, painted, sculpted, branded or carved. It could be embroidered, sewn and riveted. The ornate tooling that the Moors brought to the New World in the 1500s would not be possible with this type of leather. If chromium-tanned leather had replaced vegetable-tanned leather, leather today would be nothing more than an animal-based fabric. We would have lost the unique material that was the basis of one of our earliest art forms.

THE ARTS & CRAFTS MOVEMENT

For a short time the Arts & Crafts Movement, started by William Morris and John Ruskin in the 1860s in England, revived the craft industry in Europe and the

United States. Morris and Ruskin saw the beauty in the preindustrial age and felt that the machine age had both debased the product and the maker. They sought to restore both the status and the position of the craftsperson in society, believing that the handcrafted pieces were both morally and qualitatively superior. They were critical of the division of "craft" from "art" that had happened in the Renaissance, and felt that "art" and "craft" should be one and the same.

Leathercraft is not mentioned much in discussions of the Arts & Crafts Movement. The movement made its way to America in the 1890s, and in the early twentieth century several artist communities were established. One such community, Roycroft in East Aurora, New York, did have leather crafters in their midst. These artist communities set out to be self-sustaining environments where artists could live and work at their crafts.

WORLD WAR II AND VETERANS

The Arts & Crafts Movement died out during World War I. The Great Depression and Second World War came shortly after, and the trio put a strain on the finances and resources of both crafters and consumers in America. Leather was in short supply since it was required for the war effort. It was also used in therapeutic leatherwork programs in military hospitals, recreation centers and rehabilitation centers. Vegetable-tanned leather, with its unique ability to be tooled, carved, branded, painted and dyed, could be provided to veterans as a raw piece, and using minimal tools and without much training, they could create a useful piece of leatherwork such as a wallet.

The ability of leatherworking to make the jump from military rehabilitation and recreation to a more widespread leisure activity was recognized by Charles David Tandy on his first tour in Hawaii during World War II. Charles was the son of Dave Tandy, one of the co-founders of the Hinkley-Tandy Leather Company (today's Tandy Leather). He was introduced to the therapeutic leatherwork program while in Hawaii and wrote a letter to his father, suggesting that leather tooling might be the wave of the future. Hinkley-Tandy had been selling shoe findings (supplies to the shoe repair industry) since 1919, but with shoemakers and shoe repairers on the decline, Charles Tandy sought to expand the business in a new direction.

After the war, many returning veterans sought out craft in one form or another, and some sought out leathercraft. The Servicemen's Readjustment Act of 1944 (the GI Bill) paid for college tuition for returning veterans, and an education in crafts provided a solitary, peaceful activity where creativity reigns, much unlike the military. For many veterans, a second career in crafts was a respite from the noise and order of the service.

In 1948 the Order of the Elks, a fraternal organization, started a leather program distributing leather to veterans hospitals around the country (this is still in operation today, and they are a major source of hides to the Department of Veteran Affairs).

The postwar university students, veterans and otherwise, who chose to study craft began a new generation of working craftspeople who were educated in colleges rather than by apprenticeship programs. This "studio craft" generation of crafters, the post WWII educated craftspeople, was creating work with an educated influence, pushing the boundaries of process and purpose, giving meaning to crafts and helping to close the gap between "art" and "craft."

These university programs taught ceramics, textiles, metal or metalworking and furniture making as well as other crafts as bachelor's degree programs, but few if any taught leathercraft. For leather crafting to survive it would have to do so independently of the studio crafts movement. Leather would have to survive as a home hobby or a recreation and rehabilitation activity.

TANDY LEATHER COMPANY

In 1950, the Hinkley-Tandy Leather Company divided in two, with the Tandy Leather Company taking over the leather side of the business and Hinkley taking over the shoe findings business. Tandy quickly began to make and market home-hobby leather kits, the first of which was a baby moccasin. The kit sold for fifty cents and Tandy advertised in magazines like *Ladies' Home Journal* and *Good Housekeeping*. They sold three million pairs over the next five years, most likely to housewives.

From that first offering, Tandy steadily grew their catalog of kits. Their initial catalog, when they introduced the baby moccasin in 1951, was eight pages long. By 1954 their catalog had grown to sixty-eight pages and they were the leader in leathercraft kits, marketing their kits to schools, prisons, hospitals and sanitariums. In 1962 they became a "Junior Achievement" sponsor to ensure that the youngest generation of crafters would be familiar with leather and the leathercraft kits that they provided.

During the 1950s home-hobby kits were on the rise not just in leathercraft, but in other areas as well. These kits were inexpensive, easy to follow and let anyone with a few cents create their own "handicraft." Many craft purists and historians would ignore the home-hobby kits entirely in a discussion of craft, but in the history of leathercraft, especially leather tooling, it has its place. While on some level these kits did cause a decline in the "integrity" of craft, they also were a saving grace for vegetable-tanned/tooling leather and leathercraft. Leathercraft and tooling were not taught in schools, and chromium-tanned leather had overtaken vegetable-tanned as the leather of choice in shoe and bag manufacturing. Were it not for these kits, leather-craft easily could have died out completely.

These leathercraft kits have precut pieces, often with prepunched holes, and the thread or lace to assemble it is provided. To complete one of these kits, you only need to add artwork and assemble it. To make these kits easily accessible to home crafters, they were mass manufactured. Ironically, the factories that grew out of the Industrial Revolution and struck a blow at the working craftsperson would enable the growth in the home handicrafts market.

HOME HANDICRAFTS MARKET

The market for home handicrafts grew dramatically during the 1950s and 1960s, and this could have been, in part, due to the sentiments embodied by the "Back to the Land" movement. Fueled by disagreement with the politics at the time and the rampant consumerism espoused by most Americans, a group of "hippies" decided to leave life in the big city and move to the country to try to live off the land, supporting themselves by selling their crafts. While many of these back-to-the-landers were potters, jewelers or furniture makers, there were leatherworkers in their midst, such as Ron Swanberg. He started his leatherworking business in 1972 in West Virginia, and his work to this day has the rustic, handmade look that is reminiscent of the era of his beginnings.

The popularity of home handicrafts started to fall in the 1970s. A decrease in Scouting, school budgets, lower birthrates and an economic slump all contributed to the decline. Tandy Leather continued to make kits, but the sales and growth were lower. The number of artisans making leather shoes and bags by hand has been on the decline as well. Even the number of tanneries has

declined; currently there are fewer than a dozen, down from 250 in 1978. To find a hide of vegetable-tanned leather made in the United States, you have a choice of one, maybe two, tanneries. Commercial leather goods are made almost exclusively from chromium-tanned leather and are often manufactured overseas in India or China.

It is only the small crafters, people like you and me, who still use vegetable-tanned leather. We are the artists who want both a canvas and a construction material—something that we can decorate and shape to create a useful, durable object. When you pick up your first piece of vegetable-tanned leather, you are holding a tradition in tanning that is over four thousand years old. Now is the time to share the secrets of tanning and leatherwork that were once guarded. Those of us who take up leatherwork as a profession or a hobby should feel obliged to share what we know and what we learn. By reading this book, and by learning leathercraft, you are participating in and strengthening a living tradition.

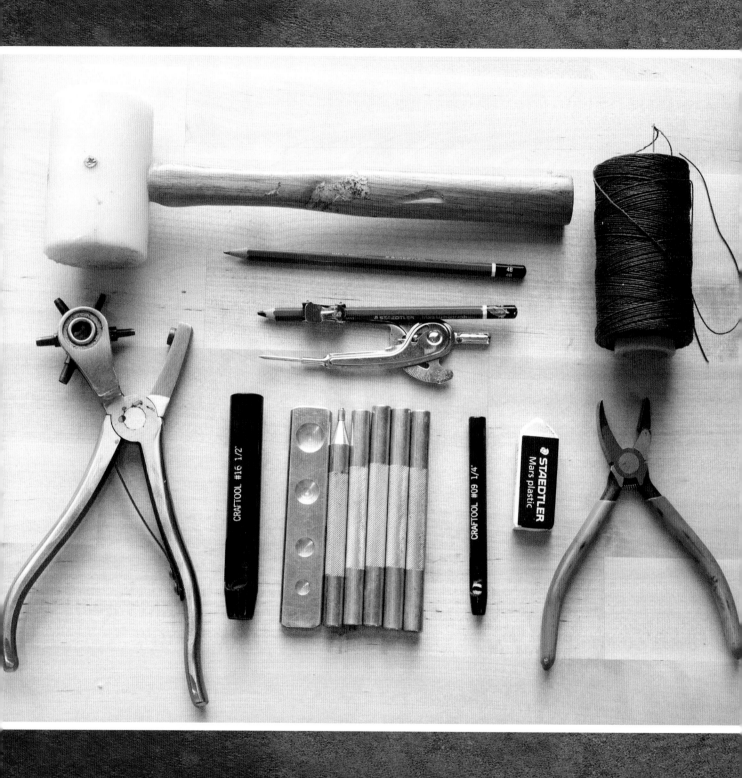

1

Tools and Materials

We are going to delve into the various tools, equipment and materials that you will need to complete the projects in this book. Keep in mind that some of these are optional: Depending on how you put pattern on your pieces, you may not need all of the items listed. Also keep in mind that many of these tools are small and inexpensive. I started with a very small budget and bought more tools as I was able to afford them. I also worked in a very small space for the first eight years—no more than 75 square feet (7 square meters) in the corner of my basement—so don't be intimidated by the length of the list. All of the essential tools will fit in a shoebox, and you can do these projects on your dining room table (with some precautions taken to avoid damaging it).

The projects in this book use vegetable-tanned tooling leather exclusively: It is untreated with dyes and oils in the factory, leaving it as close to "raw" leather as is possible for a tanned hide (a true raw hide is "rawhide," the same thing that is used for drums and dog chew toys. The tanning process is what allows the hide to become flexible so it can be used for bags, garments and various other leathercraft projects). The "vegetable" in vegetable-tanned refers to the type of substance that is used in the tanning, which is actually tree bark. Using a natural material to tan and not adding oils or dyes keeps the leather closer to its natural state, allowing all of the marks and scars to show through. It can be beautiful, but it can also be frustrating if you're looking for a completely flawless piece of leather. When you go to pick your first hide, remember that it won't be perfect. Scars, stretch marks, brands, holes and other imperfections are part of the nature of a leather hide.

Tools for Marking Leather

PENCIL, PENCIL SHARPENER AND ERASER

It's best to purchase drawing pencils for your leatherwork; they each have a hardness rating and you can choose the pencil that is best for your project. The hardness scale shows pencils that range from 6B (softest) to 6H (hardest). A pencil that is too soft can become difficult to erase from the leather, and if you use one that is too hard, it can scratch the surface of the leather, leaving a permanent mark. For general use with leatherworking, keep a 5B and a 3B on hand. The 5B will be your go-to for sketching, and the 3B is more useful for marking holes and doing tracings.

Every pencil needs an eraser. Drawing pencils typically do not have erasers attached so you'll need a separate one. There are several kinds that you can purchase, but the Staedtler Mars plastic erasers are my favorite. They remove pencil markings cleanly and do not leave a film, which can alter the dye. A good kneaded eraser will work as well, but with lots of leather scraps and shavings around they have to be changed frequently. You'll need a sharpener, too.

DRAWING COMPASS

A drawing compass is useful for marking stitch lines as well as drawing circles. Look for one that you can put your own pencil in, rather than one that comes with lead or a "wing divider" style, which is intended to scratch the surface of the leather. When you add your own pencil, you choose the pencil hardness for the compass, giving you control over how you mark the leather.

RULER, CARPENTER'S SQUARE AND CLOTH TAPE MEASURE

Although it is possible to get by with just one of these, all three serve a purpose. When you're measuring along a fixed line the ruler comes in handy since it is less cumbersome than the carpenter's square, but if you're measuring someone for a wrist cuff or a belt, the cloth tape measure is a must for wrapping around a three-dimensional figure. The carpenter's square is helpful when you are creating a pattern of your own and need to draw a rectangle, which you will need to do quite frequently.

PENCIL HARDNESS SCALE

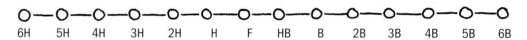

6H 5H 4H 3H 2H H F HB B 2B 3B 4B 5B 6B

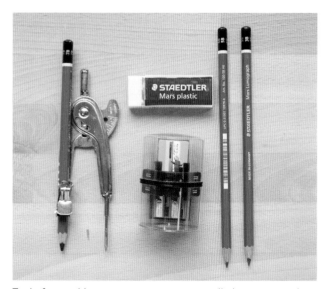

Tools for marking: compass, eraser, pencil sharpener and pencils

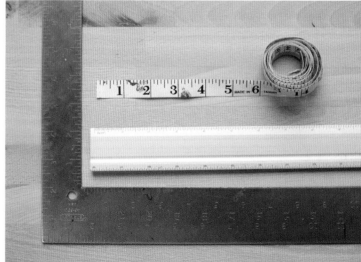

Tools for marking: carpenter's square, cloth tape measure and ruler

Cutting Tools

SCISSORS

Perhaps your most essential tool is a sharp pair of leather scissors. The Craftool Pro Super Shears and the Craftool Sure-Grip Shears are both good choices. They come out of the package very sharp and will cut your thickest leather like butter. If you get serious about leathercraft, plan on repurposing your dull shears as paper or general craft scissors and replacing them rather than having them sharpened. We have yet to find a knife sharpener that can replicate a factory blade.

KNIVES

A cutting knife can be an alternative or complement to your scissors. You can invest in a leather knife that you will sharpen to maintain the blade, or if you are cutting thinner leathers, a craft knife with a blade you can replace when it is dull. If you are comfortable using a knife, you can use it instead of your scissors to cut out your patterns. The craft knife will be useful for cutting within the leather, such as cutting out a slot for a buckle, whereas the scissors are better for cutting around edges.

ROTARY TOOL

A familiar tool for the seamstress, a third option for cutting leather is a rotary tool. This is best for cutting straight lines and requires the use of a cutting surface/mat underneath.

CUTTING SURFACE

You can cut with scissors wherever you like, although your scissors may scratch a soft surface (such as a wood floor or table) as you draw them through the leather. When you are cutting with a knife, you will want to have a rubber mat under your leather so you do not cut the surface beneath or dull your knife. You can get a black rubber mat at Tandy or another leathercraft supply store. These rubber mats also work well for setting crystal rivets.

Cutting tools: craft knife, scissors, rotary cutter and cutting surface

SPLITTERS

While not technically a cutting tool, a splitter has a blade, so we will discuss it here. A splitter or skiver is used to remove a portion of the flesh side of the leather, thereby reducing the thickness. This is something you will certainly want to do when you are working with a leather strap that needs to be folded over. Rather than folding the full thickness, split the leather to half the original thickness and then fold it over to create a neater fold and a more professional finish.

There are two types of splitters that are readily available. One is a handheld piece with a sharp blade that runs parallel to your piece. This is sometimes called a "Super Skiver." To use the handheld tool, mark the piece that you want to spilt, then place the tool on top of the flesh side of the leather, holding the leather in place with your other hand. Put the tool at a slight angle into the leather and then draw down and toward you. If your angle is too steep the skiver will not cut, and if your angle is too shallow you won't remove anything. When you are first trying the skiver, start with a small angle and work your way up as you become more comfortable with the tool. It's better to remove too little and go back for a second pass.

A tabletop splitter has a roller and must be screwed down. There is a handle on one side and a long blade. You put your leather between the blade and the roller, flesh side up, and push the handle away from you to tighten the roller. Twist the handle to lock the roller in place, and pull the leather toward you to split. Usually this style of splitter has a stopper so you can be sure you don't split the leather too thin, though again it is easier to go back and make an additional pass with the splitter if you don't take off enough than it is to try to add more leather.

Cutting tools: tabletop splitter

Cutting tools: hand skiver

Punching Tools

You have two choices for hole-punching tools: a rotary punch and a drive punch. There are advantages and disadvantages to each. If your budget allows, you will want both. If you can only afford one, start with the drive punch.

DRIVE PUNCH

A drive punch can be purchased either as a fixed tool that makes holes of one size, or as a set with one handle and interchangeable tips to create various hole sizes. For the best versatility on a budget, you want the interchangeable style. To punch a hole using a drive punch, put your leather on a punching surface with the grain side up. Then align the drive punch with the desired hole size above the leather where you want the hole, at a right angle to your surface. Hit the top of your punching tool swiftly with a mallet. For thicker leathers you might need to hit it again.

Because you are punching *through* the leather, a designated punching surface is a must. The best punching surface is actually a poly cutting board. You can use an old one or pick one up at a one-stop shopping store. They run anywhere from two to ten dollars. If you don't have one and need to do some punching, you can also use a piece of wood as the backing.

With any drive punch you will need a mallet, rubber or rawhide, to go with it. The mallet is used to hit the end of the punch and drive it through the leather. Yes, you can definitely use a hammer if you prefer (I did), but the metal on the hammer is stronger than the metal on your punch, and over time it will distort the end of your punch. Using a hammer is also much louder than using a mallet, should you have sensitive neighbors or a sleeping baby.

Drive punches come in more shapes than just circular. Noncircular punches are used for cutting decorative holes, cutting out small leather objects (keychains) or shaping belt ends. The drive punches used in this book are primarily the circular kind, used for punching holes.

ROTARY PUNCH

A rotary punch is a hand tool that has a wheel with tube punches in various sizes; you rotate the wheel to change the punch size. To use a rotary punch, rotate your desired punch size so it faces downward (toward the metal plate below) and then place the leather between the punch and the metal plate. Placing a thick (4–5 oz) piece of scrap leather or a piece of cardboard between your good leather and the metal plate will help create a cleaner punch, but you can proceed with or without this backing piece. Align the punch over the mark for your hole, and squeeze firmly. Release the handle, move the leather to the next hole mark and repeat. Unlike drive punches, rotary punches only create round holes.

Punching tools: mallet, rotary punch, fixed drive punch, drive punch with interchangable tips and punching surface

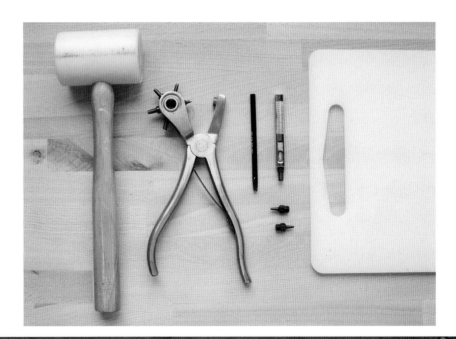

Decorative Pattern Tools

This is where my techniques start to diverge from the traditional. The following tools are traditionally used for woodworking, but if you have experience drawing or carving you will find them easy to use on leather. Best of all, they yield wonderful results.

BRANDING IRON

There are several different styles of branding iron available. You can purchase an inexpensive one with a brass tip at a craft store. Usually this style has interchangeable tips that will screw on and off, and many have no temperature control. The branding iron works by heating up a metal tip, which you can then use like a pen to burn your pattern into the surface of the leather (on the smooth grain side).

You can use the branding iron to create just the outline for your pattern and then paint it, or you can do your entire pattern with the branding iron. Because you are just charring the surface, be aware that over time the branding lines on your finished piece will crack and show the lighter leather underneath. This can be easily touched up with dye as desired, or you can leave them cracked for a beautifully worn look.

Branding leather produces smoke, so working in a well-ventilated space is important. I also recommend wearing a respirator and putting a powerful exhaust fan in your workspace (see "For Your Safety" on page 39 for more information).

CARVING TOOLS

The carving tools used in this book are actually woodworking tools as well. The best ones are the gouges, which are tools with a long U-shaped blade. You can use the gouges in thicker leather (usually 4-5 oz) to remove the surface of the leather in order to create an outline, pattern or texture. The craft knife will be useful if you need to remove a larger portion of the grain side of the leather, such as the background after you have made your carving lines. The rounded blades of the craft knife work well, and there are several different styles available.

These tools will eventually start to dull. To sharpen your gouges it is best to follow the manufacturer's instructions. The craft knife isn't easily sharpened, but the blade can be replaced and should be often to keep your cuts clean and make cutting easy.

IRON SAFETY

The tip of your branding iron or branding pen is red hot. It will take some time to cool down, so be sure you have a stand to set it on while it is cooling. Always turn your branding iron off when not in use.

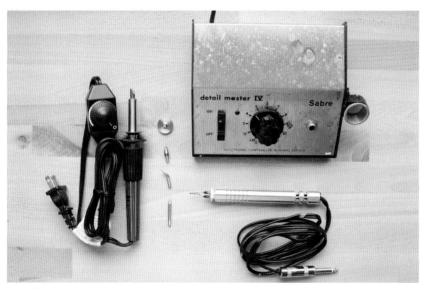
Branding iron with interchangable tips and branding iron with temperature control

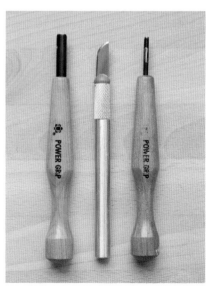
Carving tools: gouges and craft knife

Painting Supplies

Starting with a vegetable-tanned hide not only allows you to add decorative pattern, but color as well. Once you have put your pattern on the leather, the next step is the paint and then the dye. Preparing your leather and doing each step in the proper order ensures good adhesion for your paints and dyes so they won't rub off over time.

RUBBING ALCOHOL

Isopropyl rubbing alcohol (applied with wool daubers or synthetic wool sponges, more on those later) helps to open up the pores of the leather, creating a better adhesion with your paint. It also changes the way that your dyes are accepted by the leather and can act as a resist to the dyes.

PAINTS AND BRUSHES

The best acrylic paints for our projects are those made for leather. They are thinner than regular acrylic paints, making them easy to pour and custom colors easy to mix. Having a small paint tray on hand is helpful, but in a pinch you can use a plastic yogurt container lid. The paint bottles are small, but you will be surprised how long they last.

You will want a selection of various brush sizes and tip shapes; this mostly depends on your personal preference and style. You can use any artist's brushes on your leather, so feel free to choose the ones that you like best. It is best to stick with your own level of comfort and experience here since your leather has no preference about which brush you use. You can purchase brushes at your local art/craft store or online.

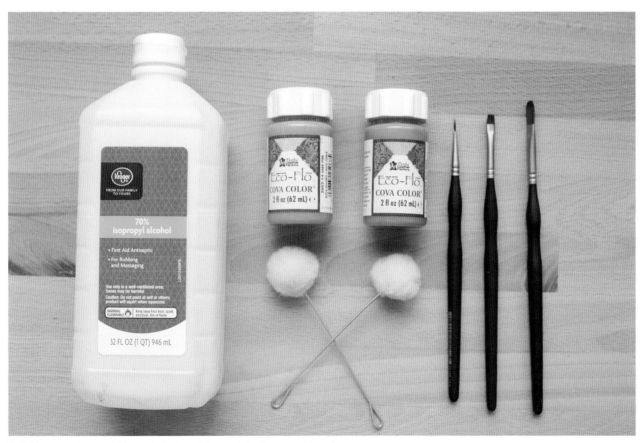

Painting supplies: rubbing alcohol, paint, wool daubers and brushes

Dyeing Supplies

After you have painted the leather you can dye it. Make sure that your piece is completely dry before beginning.

DYEING SURFACE

Your dyeing surface is important; you want something that is clean and easy to remove the dye from. The best surface is a stainless steel table, since it does not absorb the dye and can be easily cleaned with vinegar and water when you are done. You can purchase a section of stainless steel countertop to use, or you can use a large stainless steel baking sheet if you are doing smaller pieces. Another option is to cover your work surface with contractor's plastic. It comes in rolls and you can buy it online or at the hardware store. If you are working over a rug, there is no guarantee that you will be able to keep all of your dye on the table, so be sure to cover the rug as well. Even a small drop of dye will be very difficult to remove from carpet fibers. For cleaning the table after you have done your dyeing, a spray bottle with either household cleaner or distilled white vinegar and water, as well as a towel, should do the trick.

OIL

Before applying the dye, you will oil the leather. This restores some moisture to the leather and keeps it from needing to be oiled again after the topcoat has been applied. Some leathers, such as straps, will crack if you fold them tightly after they are dyed, and a coat of oil can help to prevent this. Some variation of neatsfoot oil is a good choice (pure neatsfoot oil will do just fine).

DYE

There are several types of dye: gel based (sometimes called "Antique" stains), water based and alcohol based. One of the main differences in the various stains is how they penetrate the leather. Gel dyes are superficial: They only dye the top layer of the leather and do not soak in.

Gel dyes allow the imperfections of the leather to show and give an inconsistent, antiqued look. The water- and alcohol-based stains soak into the leather, giving a deeper, darker and more consistent color, which does a better job of hiding flaws. The water- and alcohol-based dyes will show your application marks; if you apply the dye more heavily in one spot with a water or alcohol stain, the color will be noticeably darker in that spot. But though the margin of error for these dyes is slimmer, they are more durable. Since the water and alcohol dyes penetrate the surface of the leather, when the leather is scuffed or scratched it will expose more dyed leather rather than the undyed, paler natural hide beneath.

Different dyes interact differently with paint as well. Gel dyes do not affect the paint below, but water- and alcohol-based dyes do. When you apply alcohol-based dye over a painted piece, the paint will dissolve, and you can rub the paint off. A water-based dye will not dissolve the paint, but it will penetrate the leather behind it. Both water- and alcohol-based dyes will change the color of your paint as well.

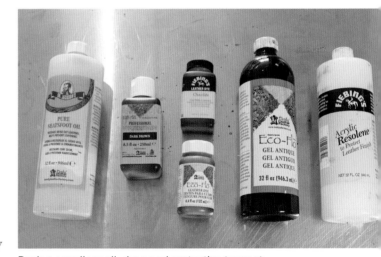

Dyeing supplies: oil, dyes and protective topcoat

SPONGES, PAPER TOWELS AND DAUBERS

There several different ways to apply dye, including sponges, paper towels and wool daubers. The wool daubers look like a wool version of a cotton ball on the end of a wire handle. They will absorb dye and work best for smaller areas when you are using either an alcohol- or water-based liquid dye. Sponges can be used for the water/alcohol-based liquid dyes as well as for the gel antique dyes. You can purchase a sponge made for leathercraft, a synthetic wool sponge, or a kitchen sponge (not the scrubber kind, just a regular one). For years, I used paper towels to do all the dyeing with antique stains since they were what I had available. They work okay for this purpose, though a sponge is much better and less wasteful.

Be sure to wear protective gloves (fitted latex, rubber or nitrile) any time you dye, as the dye will stain your hands.

Dyeing supplies: sponges, gloves, wool daubers and paper towel

DRYING RACK

When you've finished dyeing your leather, you'll need a place to dry it. You can place it directly on a clean, dry surface or, if you have the space for one, a rolling wire rack. You can pick these up at any one-stop shopping store. The advantage of a wire rack is that, even with a topcoat, your wet leather pieces will not stick to it. The rack allows air to flow around the piece and seems to speed up the drying time. Very small pieces of leather, which will easily slip off a wire rack, can dry on the table.

PROTECTIVE TOPCOAT

Protective topcoats are used to keep your dye and paint intact, and keep other unwanted things (such as water or coffee) out of your leather. As with dyes, there are several types of topcoats; your choice will depend on what you want the final product to look like and how water repellent you would like it to be. My personal favorite is Acrylic Resolene. It is a water-based finish with very little odor, so it does not require ventilation. Tandy also makes a Satin Shene and Super Shene that are low odor as well. They have different levels of gloss but are not quite as water repellent. Although it is not completely waterproof, the Acrylic Resolene will do a good job of repelling water. Tandy also sells something called "Professional Finish," which is a very water-

Projects on a drying rack

repellent topcoat and is slightly shinier than the Acrylic Resolene. This finish carries a safety warning—use it in a well-ventilated area, and if you get it on your skin, rinse immediately.

Topcoats should be applied with a synthetic wool sponge or a durable paper towel (brands such as Brawny and Bounty tend to work best because they don't leave fibers behind on the piece). Wear gloves to help protect your hands.

Hardware and Adhesives

Hardware and adhesives are both used to hold pieces of leather together, either temporarily or permanently, and they are both used in assembling your leathercraft projects. We will only use one type of adhesive, and we will be using just a few simple types of hardware: snaps, rivets, turn-lock clasps and buckles.

SNAPS

There are several different types of snaps, all serving the same purpose: as a closure for a cuff, belt, journal, bag or other item. Use snaps when you want to be able to easily attach, separate and reattach two pieces of leather using a low-profile closure. The two types that we will use are Segma snaps and Line 20 snaps. Both have four pieces, two that fit together for each side of the snap. The sides are composed of a "male" and "female" portion of the snap. The female part of the snap consists of the decorative post piece and the bowl-shaped piece. The male parts are the hidden post piece, which will be on the bottom when the snap is set, and the protruding connective piece.

The Segma snaps are smaller and work well for places where the snap is functional and needs to be relatively flat. The Line 20 snaps work best for applications on larger pieces where the small snap is out of scale, or where you need something a little stronger. Line 20 snaps also have the advantage of a longer post so they can go through thicker leather more easily, where Segma works better for thinner leather. To use the snaps, prepunch holes in the desired places and use a snap setter to join each set of pieces together.

RIVETS

Rivets are small pieces of metal that hold two (or more) pieces of leather together, or you can use them decoratively, like a nailhead trim on furniture. We will use them in the construction of some of the later projects. Rivets have two pieces, the cap and the post, that are pressed together to stay in place.

Different types of rivets are discussed in Chapter 4, where you will learn how to set them.

SNAP AND RIVET SETTERS

There are two types of snap and rivet setters that are commonly used. The first is similar to the drive punch set, except the ends of the various tools have a hole, nub or dome on the end. You will also get a tray with several different concave domes that you can put your snap or rivet in so it maintains the domed shape when you set it, rather than becoming completely flat (we will go into detail on how to do this in Chapter 4).

The second type of snap and rivet setter is a hand press. These are usually tabletop pieces (though you can purchase foot-pedal operated ones) where you press

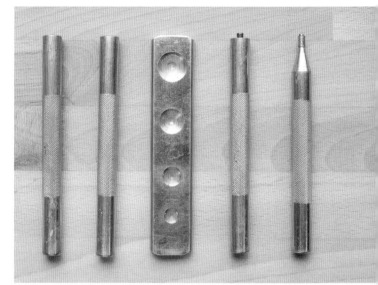

Snap and rivet setting tools

Hand press for setting rivets and snaps

Snap and rivet hand press dies

down on a lever to compress the rivet or set the snap. Each rivet or snap has a separate set of dies that are used to set it, and these dies are purchased separately. It makes the cost for this setup considerably higher. The advantage of using a setter like this is that your snaps and rivets will always be perfectly aligned.

CLASPS

There are many different types of clasps, and once you've started with a few projects and become comfortable with the materials, you will likely want to experiment with all of them. To start, we will be using turn-lock (or twist-lock) clasps. If you imagine a closure on a messenger bag, the turn locks have a metal "hole" that goes on the flap part of the bag and a twisting metal piece that goes on the body of the bag. There are two pieces that compose each portion: The flap piece has a front and back oval with the centers removed, and the bag piece has the twisting portion as well as a backing piece to keep it in place.

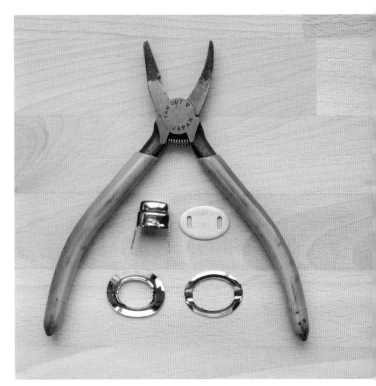

Turn-lock clasp pieces and pliers

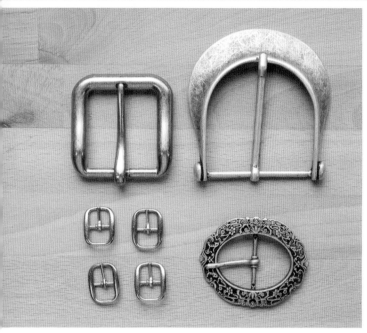

Center-bar and heel-bar buckles

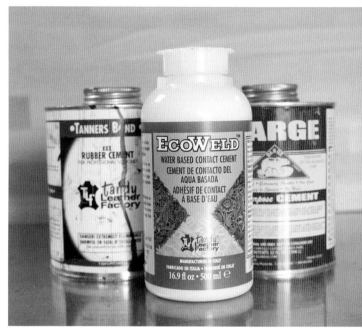

Various adhesives

A pair of pliers can come in handy when adjusting the legs on a clasp—it's not always something you can manipulate by hand.

BUCKLES

Buckles are another type of fastener, which require straps. There are three types of buckles that we will be using: center-bar and heel-bar buckles, and trophy style. The center-bar buckle is an oval, rectangle, square or circle with a bar in the middle and a tongue that moves freely. The heel-bar buckle is usually a rectangle or D shape, with the tongue (or tongues) on the straight line of the D. The trophy style has a small hook on the back of the buckle that passes through the belt hole to hold it in place.

The heel-bar and trophy-style buckles work best for belts, and the center-bar buckle works for almost any application. The advantage of the center-bar buckle is that it holds the buckle tail in place when buckled. The disadvantage is that it can be harder to buckle and unbuckle than the heel-bar buckle when you are using a thick strap, such as a belt. Using a buckle as a closure

on a bag allows flexibility because you can fasten it at multiple places along the strap, rather than only being able to fasten it in one fixed place, as is the case with a twist-lock clasp.

ADHESIVES

For the projects in this book you will use glue when you need to hold two pieces of leather together permanently. This is to facilitate stitching the pieces of leather together.

There are many different types of glue with different purposes that you can use for leather. The glue used in this book is designed to hold a permanent bond. If you have a well-ventilated area, you can use Barge Cement. Barge has a strong odor and carries one of those State of California warnings on the package that states it can cause cancer or birth defects. Your best ventilation is outdoors, so in a temperate climate a covered outdoor space is a good option. If you are in a space without adequate ventilation, Tandy Leather makes EcoWeld Water-Based Contact Cement, which has no odor or warnings associated with it.

Stitching Needs

Hand sewing is a beautiful and durable way to assemble your piece of leather art. The advantage of hand sewing is that it is easier to learn than machine sewing and does not require an initial investment in a machine. It's very durable, and it also allows your leatherwork to be repaired more easily. Leather is not self-healing, so if you machine sew a piece of leather and have to rip a seam out, or repair a seam on an old finished piece, the holes from the original stitching will always be there. When you hand sew, your holes are carefully marked and punched by hand. If your thread ever breaks, the larger-size hole makes it easy to resew your piece using the original holes.

THREAD

A waxed thread will work well for all of your hand-stitching needs, but the colors that are available specifically for leatherwork are pretty boring: black, brown, tan. You can also use a waxed polyester thread (1mm works well) that is marketed for beading. This comes in wonderful colors and is a great way to add another layer of artistry to your piece. When you go to stitch your piece, you will first mark and punch all of your holes with the smallest punch (1⁄16" [1.6mm], or size 00) and then stitch through the prepunched holes.

NEEDLES

Use leathercraft needles for hand stitching your pieces. They look like giant sewing needles with a very large eye for passing the thicker thread through. There are sharp needles and needles with a dull point. The dull ones are perfect for stitching through leather alone with prepunched holes because you won't accidentally puncture the leather, or yourself, while stitching. When you are stitching through leather and something else, such as a zipper, you will want a sharp-point needle to puncture the other fabric.

Waxed thread and leathercraft needles

Types of Hides

When you go to look for your first hide, you'll find there are several different "cuts" from the cow. There is a side, which is the largest and is cut from the entire side of a cow. You can also get a shoulder, either single or double (single being the smaller of the two) that is cut from the shoulders of the cow. Even though leather is often priced by the square foot or meter, most places do not cut the hides for you, so you will want to choose the piece that best suits your project and leather needs.

Hides are almost always marked with square footage, which can be a helpful indicator. Just remember that when you are cutting your piece there will likely be waste along the edges, as well as some spots in the center of the hide you will want to avoid due to scarring or other imperfections. If you have calculated carefully and know that you need 20 square feet (1.9 square meters) for a project, you will want to buy a hide that is bigger, maybe 25 square feet (2.3 square meters), since not every square foot (or meter) of the hide will be usable. You may cut around imperfections, thin spots and uneven edges, creating scrap. Those scraps are good for small projects, though, so hang onto them.

Hide diagram

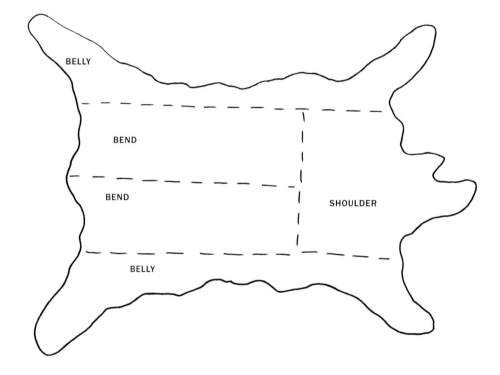

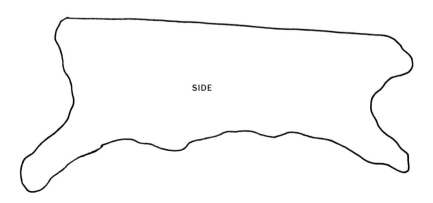

FLESH VS. GRAIN SIDE

The hide has two sides. The top is a smooth surface, called the "grain" side of the leather, and the rough underside is called the "flesh" side. When you see leather referred to as "full grain" or "top grain" it means that the grain side of the leather is intact. An example of leather that is not full grain, or top grain, is suede. Suede is made from what is called a "split" of leather, where the top portion of the hide, the grain, is removed from the leather, leaving the flesh side and the interior. This is the weaker portion of the leather, so when you see "full grain" or "top grain" it means that the leather used has the strongest portion intact. For the projects in this book we will use only full-grain, vegetable-tanned tooling leather. When you start adding patterns, we will be doing all of this on the grain side of the leather.

LEATHER WEIGHTS

Leather comes in a variety of weights listed in ounces. The ounce weight refers to the weight of the leather per square foot. Different projects require different weights, but in general terms, the lighter-weight leathers are more desirable for items that should soften up with use. If you're constructing a bag that you would like to become relaxed and broken-in with use, opt for a lighter-weight leather (2–3 oz). If you want a messenger bag that will hold its shape when broken in, opt for a heavier leather (4–5 oz or 5–6 oz). Lighter leathers also work better for items that need to fold, such as pouches and tablet cases.

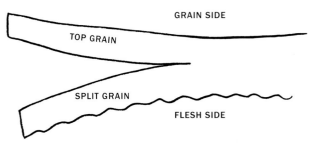

Two sides of a hide

ORGANIZE SCRAPS BY WEIGHT

Save your scraps by weight! Rather than digging through a box of scraps to find the correct type of leather, create various bins or boxes marked for each leather thickness. Then put your scrap in the appropriate bin as you cut it off the hide for easy access when you are making small projects.

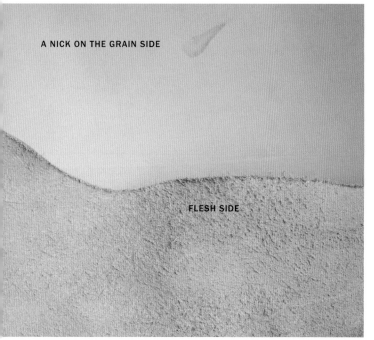

A NICK ON THE GRAIN SIDE

FLESH SIDE

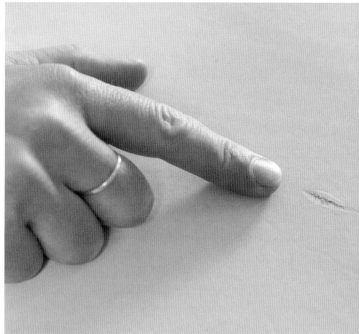

A cut in the grain side of a hide. Avoid it when using the hide.

PROBLEM SPOTS

When you're ready to unroll the hides at the leather store, you will want to take your time and go over each carefully. Look for problem spots: Scars and stretch marks will be the most obvious. Most sides will have a brand on them somewhere (shoulders should not). The brand itself is not an inherent problem—you can easily dye it and generally it isn't accompanied by a thin spot—but you might not want to have it as part of your piece. Stretch marks are the same. If you are using a gel antique stain, these will likely show through slightly. If this is okay with you, a stretch-marked side may be suitable. If not, you can keep searching for something that is cleaner.

On the grain side the biggest problems are spots where the leather is marked and the mark has a different texture, since these will show up when using a gel antique stain. They can look like cracks or nicks in the leather, or like freckles, and a spot like this will be visible on your finished piece when using a gel antique stain or

light water-based stain. The darker water/alcohol-based stains will hide these marks.

If the grain side looks good, you will also want to look for thin spots. Run your hands over the front and back of the leather simultaneously. You may feel some spots where the leather gets thinner. Sometimes this happens quickly, and it can happen anywhere on the piece, although it usually happens toward the edges. Again, thin spots can be fine as long as you avoid them when you are cutting your hide.

Next, take a good look at the back. More problematic than the general variations in thickness are isolated spots that look like nicks in the leather. These spots that cut into the flesh side of the leather create a weak point in the hide, and you will want to work around them when you are cutting out your piece. If you accidentally cut your piece with one in the middle and hit it with a branding iron or carving knife, your tool can go right through. If you buy a piece with one of these thin spots, mark it with a pencil on the grain side when you get home so you can be sure to cut around it.

Holes in a hide. The large hole also has scarring below it, which may indicate a thin spot on the back of the hide.

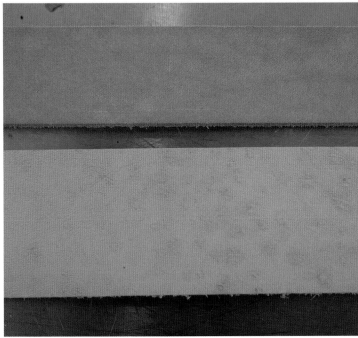

Top: Belt strap discolored by sunlight
Bottom: Belt strap with "freckling"

CHECKLIST FOR CHOOSING THE HIDE

What choosing the hide comes down to, in almost any instance, is what looks good to you. However, here are the things you'll want to look at, and look for.

1. First choose the weight: Do you want a heavier leather that will hold its shape? Or a lighter leather that is easier to fold and will get soft and relaxed with use?
2. How big a hide do you want? A shoulder? A side? Remember that you will need to cut your biggest pattern piece continuously out of the hide, so take a tape measure if necessary.
3. Does the hide have scars, stretch marks, freckles and other superficial imperfections? How is this going to impact your finished piece?
4. Is the hide relatively uniform in thickness? Are there any major divots on the flesh side that would create weak spots?

Once you've found a hide that you like, it's time to check out and get back to your studio— we're going to make something!

STORING HIDE

To store your hide between projects, roll it up with the flesh side out and keep it away from sunlight. Sunlight can discolor the leather, and although you will dye it eventually, the discoloration will show through, especially with some of the lighter dyes.

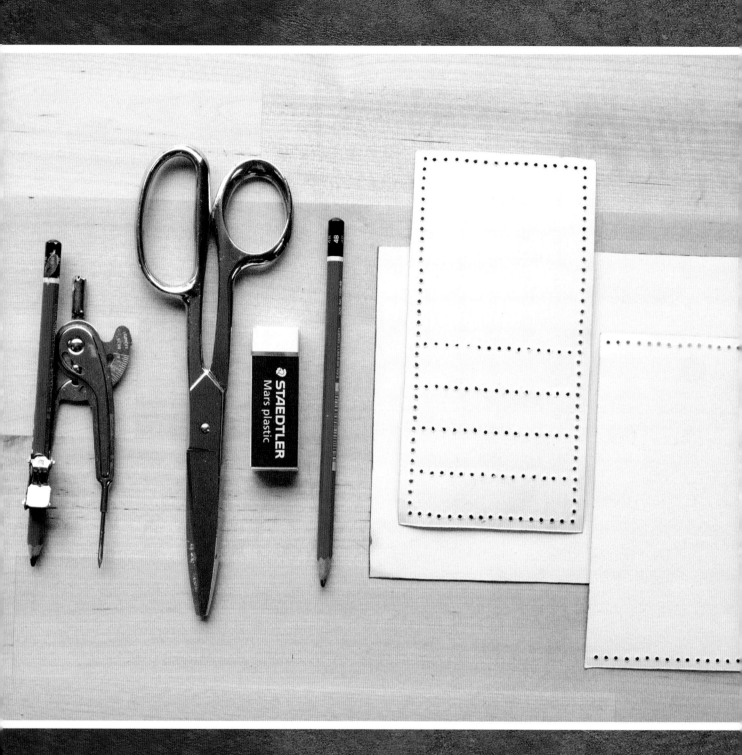

Working With Patterns

If you have worked with patterns in sewing before, you have a little bit of a head start, but only a small one. There are a few similarities between leatherworking and sewing, but there are also a lot of differences. First of all, the patterns used with leather are on a much thicker paper than the thin tissue that you use with fabric. This is because instead of pinning the pattern in place, you will hold it or use weights to keep it stable. Then, instead of cutting around the edges of the pattern, you will trace the pattern with a pencil. Depending on the pattern you may also be marking holes for stitching, rivets or snaps. And don't plan on cutting multiple layers of leather at one time because you can't pin the leather (you'd leave permanent holes in it), and it doesn't fold well. Tracing and cutting one piece at a time is your best bet.

The biggest difference between leatherwork patterns and sewing patterns is how they go together. Fabric is generally thinner and more flexible than tooling leather, so stitching it right sides together and then turning it inside out is easy. Not so with leather. Leather does have one distinct advantage, though: Since leather doesn't fray the way fabric does, you can easily stitch pieces of leather together leaving the edge "raw" (not hemmed or serged) and still achieve a finished look.

Preparing and Tracing Your Pattern

Before you cut your leather, you first need to cut out your pattern. Begin with a provided pattern, and then after practicing with it, move into creating your own patterns. Use cardstock when copying your patterns, especially if you plan on using it multiple times (photocopy paper is fine but will wear quickly).

Using sharp paper scissors, cut along the solid lines of the pattern. Using your hole punch and a piece of thick scrap leather behind it as backing, punch the holes as shown on the pattern, using the same size punch. If you are not sure of the punch size, start with a small one and then work your way up; it's easier to make a hole bigger than smaller. If the hole is in the center of the pattern and you cannot reach it with a rotary punch, use a drive punch. If the pattern has a slot, cut it carefully with a craft knife.

Put your leather on a large, flat, clean surface. Even a small piece of scrap leather underneath the leather can cause a problem when you are tracing your pattern, cutting or adding pattern to your leather, so it is important to maintain a clean cutting surface at all times.

Check your leather carefully for thin spots, nicks, brands or other imperfections that you may not want in your piece. It is always up to you how you would like your finished piece to appear, so if you find an imperfection that you don't mind, go ahead and include it. If you prefer a smoother piece of leather, cut around it and save the imperfect leather for your scrap bin or a part of your project that is not visible, such as the inside of a journal cover. Thin spots and gouges, however, you should always cut around; they are a weak spot in the leather and will weaken your finished project.

Place your pattern faceup on the leather. If you have a few small weights, put these on the pattern to help hold it in place, but be careful not to obscure your view of the pattern. Trace the edges using a soft pencil (5B works best). Once you have the edges traced, mark the holes and any slots with your pencil as well.

If your project involves multiple pieces, trace all of them onto the leather at the same time. For ease of cutting, leave at least ¼" (6mm) between the tracings. As you get more experienced cutting leather you may be able to move them closer together, but at least to begin with, cutting a thin strip of leather is not always easy.

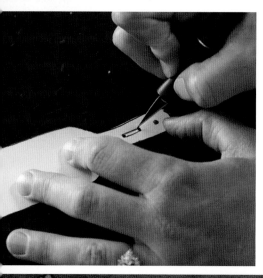

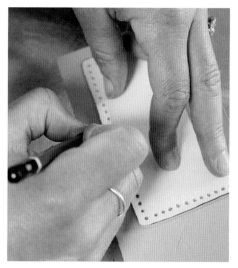

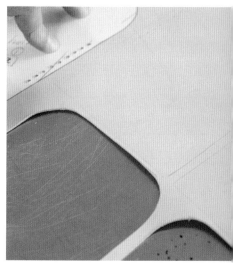

Cutting Your Leather

Once you have traced your pattern, get your sharpest leather shears (or cutting knife) and carefully cut along the solid lines. If you are cutting a small piece out of a large hide, it's helpful to cut a rough outline of the piece, leaving at least ¼" (6mm) on all sides. For instance, if you're cutting a cuff, cut a rough oval or rectangle around the cuff to free it from the hide. Then you can hold it in your hands, and using your scissors, cut carefully along the lines that you drew. It will be easier for you to see and control the scissors if you are not cutting on the table, and the rigidity of the leather, combined with the markings on the piece, make cutting in midair possible.

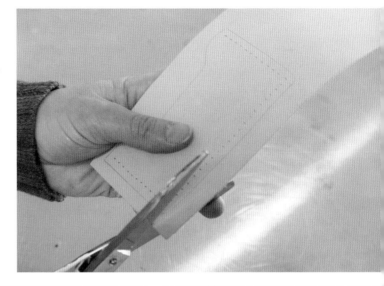

Once you have cut the outline, you will then punch the holes using either a drive or a rotary punch, or a combination of the two. If you are using a drive punch, put your leather on a punching surface first, (such as a poly cutting board) grain side up. Then align the drive punch with the desired hole size above the leather where you want the hole, at a right angle to your surface, and hit it swiftly with the mallet. For thicker leathers, you might need to hit it again.

If you are using a rotary punch, rotate your desired punch size so it faces downward (toward the metal plate below) and then place the leather between the punch and the metal plate. Using a thick (4–5 oz) piece of leather placed between your good leather and the metal plate will help create a cleaner punch, but you can do it with or without this leather backing piece. Align the punch over the mark for your hole, and squeeze firmly. Release the handle, move the leather to the next hole mark and repeat.

If there are any slots in your pattern, such as a space for a buckle, you can either cut these with your knife or a hole punch and craft knife. To cut them using a knife, put your leather on a cutting surface (either a rubber mat or poly cutting board) and hold it firmly with one hand. With the other hand, carefully draw the knife through the leather surface and cut the shape. When cutting curves, you might find it easier to move the leather than to try to get your knife to turn the corners.

Rather than cutting the entire slot by hand, you can give yourself a head start by punching the ends with a drive or rotary punch. To do this, choose a punch size that has the same diameter as the width of the slot. Punch a hole on each end of the slot, then cut along the marked edges of the slot with your knife, connecting the holes.

FOLLOW A PRACTICE PATTERN

Now that you have read about all the basics of leathercraft patterns, it's time to practice using them. This practice pattern will give you the opportunity to try out some of the techniques you just read about and work out any potential kinks before starting on your first official project. Save this practice piece because we will use it to practice other techniques later on.

1 Copy and cut out the pattern shown, making sure you punch any holes and cut the slots as they are marked.

2 Trace the pattern onto the leather.

3 Cut the leather.

4 Punch the holes. Notice that the holes are different sizes. The smaller holes will be used for stitching, and the larger holes will be used for rivets and snaps.

5 Cut the slots and punch the holes. Now take a look at your piece: Pay attention to the lines and how straight you were able to cut them, and whether the holes are on target or if you can still see the original pencil marks where the holes were supposed to be. If your lines are not straight you might want to practice your cutting again. You can do this easily by drawing a few lines with a ruler on scrap leather and cutting them out.

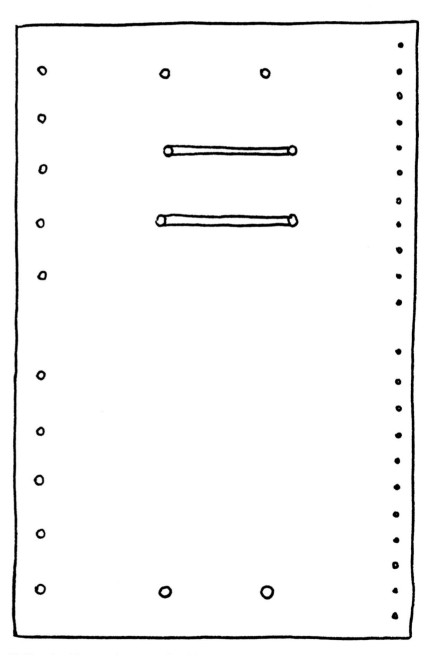

We'll make this sample pattern for this exercise.

CREATE A POUCH PATTERN

Now that you've cut one premade pattern, it's time to make one of your own! We will start with a very simple pouch with no closures. Save this piece so you can use it for practice with dyeing and adding a surface (decorative) pattern.

1 Using a piece of cardstock to create your pattern, draw a rectangle. To make a pouch for pens or glasses, a 7" × 3½" (17.8cm × 8.9cm) rectangle will work well.

2 Once you have drawn the rectangle, cut it out using your paper scissors. Rounding the edges slightly on the pattern and on your finished piece will help the corners wear better; points tend to bend and lose their shape over time.

3 Take your drawing compass and set it at ¼" (6mm) width. Place the point of the compass on the edge of your pattern and the pencil on the pattern itself. Drag the point along the edge, creating a line ¼" (6mm) in from the edge of the pattern. (Figure 1)

4 The line you just created is where you will mark your stitching holes. Measure the distance between your holes or mark them freehand. You can choose the distance between your holes, but for stitching no more than ⅜" (1cm) is best. On a small piece, closer stitching holes spaced between ¼" (6mm) and ⅛" (3mm) apart will look more to scale. (Figure 2)

If you would like your pattern to be symmetrical, fold your pattern piece in half along the line of symmetry and mark holes on one side only. Punch the holes using your rotary or drive punch and a backing sheet, then fold the pattern along

A NOTE ABOUT PATTERN SYMMETRY

When you are creating a finished leather piece that has a front and back that are the same, such as a pouch, you can make the holes on your pouch symmetrical or you can make them asymmetrical. Both options work; the only difference is that when you are tracing your pattern to the leather you will need to trace one with the pattern up and one with it flipped upside down if your pattern is not symmetrical.

your fold line and, using a pencil, mark these holes on the other side of the pattern. Punch the marked holes. (Figure 3)

5 Trace your pattern onto the leather. Since your pouch will have a front and back, you will want to trace it twice. If your pattern is not symmetrical, trace it onto the leather once with the pattern faceup and the second time facedown.

6 Cut out the pieces.

7 Punch the holes using your rotary or drive punch on size 00 (¹⁄₁₆" [1.6mm]) (used for stitching).

Now you are done. Take a look at your two pieces and try aligning them with the flesh sides of the leather together. Hold them up to the light to see if your holes align. How did you do?

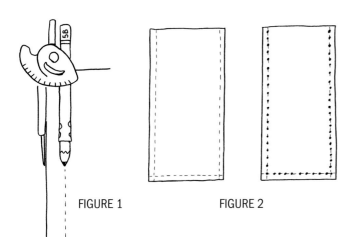

FIGURE 1   FIGURE 2

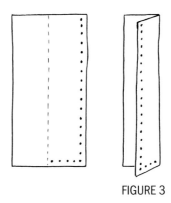

FIGURE 3

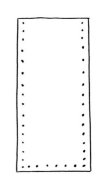

Decorative Techniques

Traditional leather tooling involves mallets and a set of stamps and tools. To create a surface (decorative) pattern using traditional tooling, you place the stamp on the leather, hit it with the mallet to compress the leather and repeat (again and again and again) until you have created a relief pattern. It's beautiful and quite time-consuming. It's also limiting. In order to compress the leather, you need a thick piece. The thinner pieces just don't have enough substance to compress, and your tool will go right through.

When I began to work with leather, I didn't know what any of the stamps in the leathercraft store were used for, and my knowledge hasn't come that far since. I did, however, have some wood carving tools, a branding iron and an adventurous spirit. I developed my own decorative techniques that I will share with you now.

Branding Leather (Pyrography)

Leather burning is certainly not something that I invented. You can do a quick image search online to find a number of images showing leather pyrography. At the time I am writing, most of the images you will find don't use much, if any, color. You can use pyrography to create texture and pattern on the surface, just as traditional tooling is used, or you can use it as a simple outline, a guide for your painted elements. The latter is how I have used pyrography, and how we will use pyrography in this book.

The only tools you need for leather burning are leather, a pencil, an eraser and a burning tool. The pencil and eraser are actually optional. You can buy a very basic burning tool at a craft store, or you can purchase a more complex one. The simple ones have small metal tips that screw in and out, and no temperature control. The more sophisticated units have temperature control and interchangeable burning pens, or at least pens with interchangeable tips. I prefer the interchangeable pens, since you don't have to wait for the tip to cool in order to change it. The one that I have used for many years is the Detail Master Excalibre, which has two interchangeable pens with heat control.

To start branding, you will want to first practice on a bit of scrap.

Any scrap will work; branding is not picky about the thickness of leather you use since it affects only the very surface of the leather. Get a feel for your branding iron so you know how it will behave when you start to brand your piece. Turn it on and use it on a piece of scrap leather as you would a normal pen: make some lines, some swirls, try writing your name. Make sure your motions include both pushing and pulling the branding iron tip to see how it changes the line as it moves toward or away from you.

If you have temperature control, try changing the temperature to see how it affects the way you use the branding iron, and how the branding iron marks the leather. I like to run my branding iron rather hot because it creates a darker line and deeper brand. Branding on the hotter settings does require that you move more quickly, since if you keep your branding iron in one place on a hot setting, you could burn a hole in your leather.

Once you've experimented with the temperature settings, change the tip, or the pen, to see the various levels

CAUTION
. . . .
It has been said before but it warrants repeating: branding iron tips are red hot. Do not touch them while they are on or cooling (this may take a while after they have been turned off). Also be sure to keep all materials, especially flammable ones, away from the tip of the branding iron. If you touch the iron to a piece of paper, the paper will catch on fire. And no, this is not an invitation for a little experimentation.

of detail. When you're just getting started you might want to make yourself a little card with the various tip names written out and a sample line from each. This will help you keep track of the tips and give you a better chance of choosing the right one for your project on the first try.

When you feel like you have thoroughly explored the various tips and temperature settings on your branding iron, get another piece of scrap leather. This time draw a pattern or image onto the leather that you will then brand. Using a 5B pencil, or one of similar hardness, draw your pattern directly on the grain side of the leather. If you are relatively experienced in drawing, you can do a quick outline and then fill in the details while you are doing the branding. Just remember that there is no eraser on the branding iron: Once the line is there, it is permanent. After you have your pattern outlined, turn on your branding iron and brand the pattern.

Next, take the piece of leather you used in your pattern-making practice and draw a design on it, then brand the design. Keep in mind when choosing and planning your design that most branding tips will not create a line finer than a medium felt-tip pen. You can get detail tips on the branding irons with interchange-able pens, but the craft-store style is more limited.

You may notice that the handpiece of your branding iron is starting to get hot. At this point it is best to take a break, let it cool off and then start again when it is completely cool. You risk dropping the handpiece if it becomes too hot for you to hold, and this could cause injury.

If your branding iron starts to become sticky (the lines become less smooth, and it feels as though it is dragging in the leather), take a piece of fine sandpaper (200-grit) and rub it over the tip. You can use it to sharpen the point of your branding tool so it will create a finer line, but be sure to use it sparingly since excessive sanding will shorten the life of your tool.

FOR YOUR SAFETY
· ·

When you brand a piece of leather you are burning it, creating smoke. I do not know the potential effects that long-term exposure can have. It is best to take every precaution when branding and work in a well-ventilated space. Because smoke rises, if you have the means and ability, put a very powerful exhaust fan at the height of your branding iron where you are doing your work. Turn the fan on high; this will pull the smoke out before it has a chance to rise above your face.

You should also wear a respirator. Look for a respirator that protects you from vapors, not just particles, since the smoke is very fine. It's not the most fashionable piece, but will certainly help to preserve your lung function if you make a habit of leather burning.

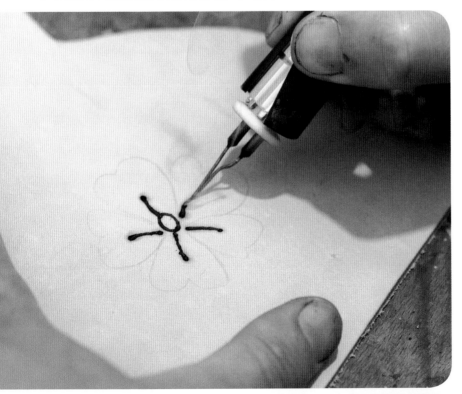

Carving Leather

The carving we will be doing uses wood tools (gouges) and craft knives. These tools work well for thicker leather and give a very different look than traditional leather tooling does because you are actually removing a portion of the surface of the leather. The minimum thickness for carving is about a 4–5 oz weight (.88mm–1.2mm thick). Gouges and craft knives are relatively inexpensive, and you will only need a few to create a variety of different looks. Invest in two gouge sizes initially, as well as one curved craft knife blade. Good gouges to start with are the Shinwa 3mm #9 gouge and the 6mm #8 gouge.

GOUGING

To practice with your wood carving tools, first pick a thick piece of scrap leather (at least 4–5 oz). Going a little heavier on your test piece will allow you to get a feel for the tools and have a cushion if you go too deep. For your carving practice, draw an outline to see how well you can follow the lines. Creating the line you intend with a carving tool is much more difficult, and less like drawing, than it is with a branding iron.

Rest the thin part of the tool against the crook of your thumb just as you would hold a pen, and place the cutting surface at about a 45-degree angle to the leather. Rest your hand on the leather to stabilize it and, pushing gently away from you, move your tool through the leather to gouge out a line. To turn corners, you can either turn your tool, or turn the leather underneath your tool. Turning the leather is often easier when you are working with a smaller piece. Turning the tool can be awkward because the carving gouges only work when you are pushing them away from you, and usually leather carves more easily in one direction than another.

Practice on scrap leather with all of the gouges that you have, and try wetting the leather first with a sponge or paper towel to feel the difference this makes in the movement of your tool and the ease with which you can carve. While the water may make it easier to carve, it does make it harder to see any pencil marks on the leather. Wetting the leather works best on the 7–8 oz or thicker leathers.

CAUTION

These tools are very sharp. At some point, you will probably cut yourself with them. Take precautions when using these tools as you would any sharp knife, and be especially careful to keep these tools away from children.

CARVING

Once you have gotten a feel for the gouges, it is time to try the craft knife. Fit it with the curved blade to help remove some of the "background" of the pattern. I used this technique often when I first started, to make my belts look more like wood. Removing the background with a craft knife creates an uneven appearance, like rough-cut wood.

First, create your outlines using your gouge. Then, placing your craft knife at a slight angle to the leather where the edge of your outline is, slowly push the blade toward the area of leather you wish to remove. You can go back and remove more if you'd like, so start small at first. Repeat this same motion, always starting on your outline and moving into the background area, removing more leather each time until all of the background has been removed. It won't be perfectly smooth, but this is part of the charm.

HOW TO MAKE A TRANSFER

For particularly complex patterns or if you prefer to do your drawing on another piece of paper first, create a carbon transfer to transfer your image from a sheet of paper to the leather. To do this, you can use carbon paper and place it between the grain side of the leather and your paper and trace over the lines with a relatively hard pencil (anything between a 2B and a 2H is fine). Or, if you don't have carbon paper, you can take a soft pencil and, using the side, cover the back of the paper with pencil marks where your pattern is. Then flip it over and align it on your leather where you would like the pattern to be. Trace the pattern lines using your pencil. Remove the paper and see the pattern you've just copied. This works well for transferring logos, too.

If you're not confident in your ability to draw your own patterns on the leather, there are many resources online for free and pay-per-image art. Use the carbon transfer method to transfer these images to your leather.

Adding Color

One element that has always set my leatherwork apart from the masses is the use of color. I love bright, bold colors, simple patterns and a folk-art style. The use of paint and various dye colors can add a distinctive element to your work as well, and the ability to add permanent color is another advantage of using vegetable-tanned leather.

When you add color it is important to add all of your paint first, before you add dye. Painting directly on undyed leather keeps the colors truer since they are being applied on a light-colored surface rather than a dark one. The paints are not completely opaque, so the color underneath will show through. Just like painting on a dark wall, it will take more layers of paint to create a true color on a dark piece of leather than on a light one.

PREPARING THE LEATHER FOR COLOR

Before you add any paint you need to prepare the leather. Use your eraser to remove any remaining pencil marks, either from when you were cutting out your leather, or from when you were branding/carving your pattern. A stray pencil mark will likely blend in with darker colors, but it will definitely show with lighter ones.

Once you have removed all of the pencil marks, dip a wool dauber or synthetic wool sponge in your rubbing alcohol. Rub the wool dauber across your piece in either circular or crosshatched motions until the entire piece has been lightly wetted. Isopropyl rubbing alcohol helps open the pores of the leather, giving the paint better adhesion. The rubbing alcohol can also, oddly, act as a resist to the dyes (all types), which is why you want to cover the entire piece in nonlinear motions. If the alcohol does not cover the surface entirely, the untreated parts can create stripes in your finished piece. These will show up during the dyeing process.

PAINTING YOUR PIECE

We will use acrylic leather paints for these projects. They are easy to work with and they clean up with water. When applied properly to a prepared vegetable-tanned leather surface, they are permanent.

Dye colors: undyed (1), blue water based (2), antique brown gel (3), antique saddle tan gel (4), chocolate brown water based (5), antique black gel (6)

Apply rubbing alcohol to leather.

Apply paint in thin, flat layers.

To begin, you need paints, a brush (or several brushes depending on the needs of your project), a paper towel and possibly a small dish to mix your paint in. You have a lot of options when it comes to applying paint to leather. Use paintbrushes, your fingers, a sponge or a stamp. Each brush, and each style of brush, will give you a different look and a different level of control over your paint. It is up to you to decide the look of your piece, and to determine the necessary paintbrush size based on the level of detail of your project.

Before you start, wet your brush in your water and then dry it off with your paper towel. Wetting the brush before you start helps to loosen the bristles, but you don't want to put a dripping wet brush in your paint or on your piece. If there is too much water on your brush, drops of water will get on your piece and mix with the paint, causing it to run.

Apply the paint in thin, flat layers. Avoid putting globs of paint or thick layers on your piece as these can easily peel or chip off once your piece is finished. Instead, to create a solid, saturated paint color, apply multiple light layers letting the paint dry between layers. Most paints will cover in one layer, and no more than three layers should be necessary for any colors.

If you are mixing colors on your paint tray (or yogurt lid), mix less paint than you think you will need. Leather requires very little paint to cover, and paint out of the jars does not store well. You can always mix a little more paint if you run out.

If you have painted before, in any medium, painting leather will feel like second nature to you. Practice on scrap if you want, or take out your practice piece from the pattern you made in Chapter 2 and paint it.

The deer head has two layers of white paint while the ears have one layer of white paint.

FIXING MISTAKES

Leather is very unforgiving at every step, paint included. If you make a mistake while painting your piece, you can remove it by dipping a wool dauber in rubbing alcohol and rubbing it over the paint that you wish to remove. The alcohol acts as a solvent to the paint and will remove it. You may, however, take off a little more paint than you wish, requiring you to repaint as needed.

DYEING YOUR PIECE

Although it might be somewhat counterintuitive, you will dye the leather after you paint it. When you dye your piece you will change the color of all of the visible unpainted vegetable-tanned leather. Depending on the dye that you are using, you may also change the color of your paints.

Before you start the dyeing process, make sure your paint is completely dry. Once the paint is dry, take a paper towel or synthetic wool sponge and apply some neatsfoot oil to the grain side of your project. The neatsfoot oil helps to soften the leather and keeps the piece supple.

After you have oiled your piece you are ready to start dyeing. Make sure your work surface is appropriate for this part of the project. You will certainly get dye on your work surface and may get it on the floor: cover anything you want to keep stain free. A stainless steel surface is best, but you can also cover a table with contractor's plastic and do your dyeing there.

APPLYING GEL (ANTIQUE) DYES

These are my favorite dyes. I use them for most everything because they allow the colors to remain true, and give a beautiful, naturally distressed look to the leather. They are also easy to apply. A sponge is the best applicator for a gel dye. You can purchase a sponge made for leathercraft, or you can use a regular kitchen sponge (not the scrubber kind, just a regular one).

If you are using a kitchen sponge, rinse it thoroughly before starting. The substance that keeps the sponge from drying out in the package can affect the color of your dye. Even if it's a sponge you've used before, rinsing is important. Squeeze and rub the sponge under warm running water. After rinsing, give the sponge one good squeeze to get the excess water out, leaving it slightly damp. This will help your dye go a little further and prevent your piece from getting dark too quickly.

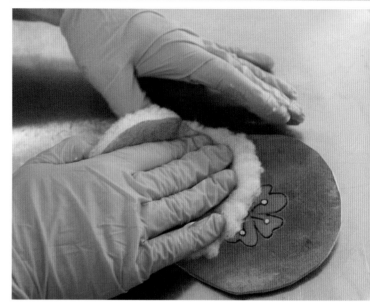
Apply neatsfoot oil.

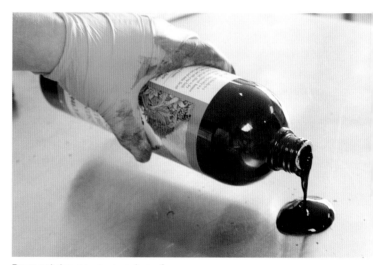
Pour gel dye on your work surface.

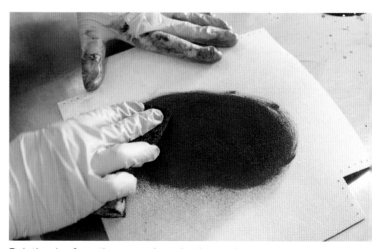
Rub the dye from the center in a circular motion.

WEAR GLOVES

Always wear gloves when you are dyeing. The dyes change the color of the leather, and they will definitely change the color of your hands. Fitted latex, rubber or nitrile gloves work best and you can pick them up at the drugstore, one-stop shop or craft store.

When you are ready to dye, pour the gel dye on your work surface. Having the gel at the ready helps expedite the dyeing process; no need to pour the gel out of the container as you go. Place your piece facedown (you will dye the back of your piece first) and dip your sponge in the dye. Put your sponge in the center of your piece and rub the dye onto the surface of the leather using circular motions. You can, and should, work quickly but carefully. With the gel dyes, a drip or a drop of dye left in one spot will form a dark area quickly.

Add more dye to your sponge as needed and continue dyeing your piece, working toward the edges and leaving the areas where there are holes for last. Do not apply so much dye that there is a layer resting upon the leather; if you can see excess dye, wipe it off with your sponge or a dry paper towel. When you have finished dyeing the back, pick up your piece and dye the edges, adding more dye to the sponge as needed. When the edges are done, put the piece on your work surface and dye the front.

When you dye the front you will likely not need to add much, if any, dye to your sponge since there will be some remaining from dyeing the back and edges. Start by running your sponge quickly over the places where the dye came through from the back to prevent any dark spots (this usually happens around the edges and at the holes). Then, work the rest of the piece, again using circular motions and adding more dye as needed. Try not to leave excess dye on the piece, as it can be hard to remove when you add the topcoat. If you think you have too much dye, wipe it off with a clean part of your sponge or a paper towel.

When you are done dyeing your piece, set it on your drying rack or a clean surface to dry. If you are dyeing additional pieces of the same color, use your sponge to wipe off any excess dye on the surface of your table to avoid getting it on your next piece. If you are dyeing with a new color, be sure to thoroughly clean your work surface between colors.

ASSIGN SPONGES

To keep your sponges straight for use with specific dye colors, cut one, two, three or four corners off of them to indicate which dye each should be used with which sponge. You can avoid having to use a new sponge each time. Throw sponges away when they are losing chunks and have gone flat.

Apply dye to the edges.

Dye came through stitch holes while dying the back.

Run the sponge over areas where the dye came through.

Apply dye to the back first, using a circular motion.

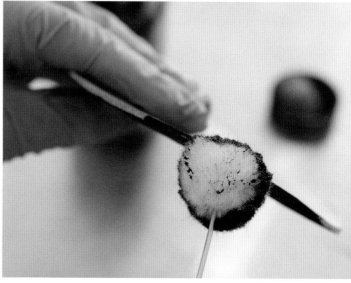

Apply dye to the edges.

ALCOHOL- AND WATER-BASED LIQUID DYES

Alcohol- and water-based liquid dyes can be applied with a sponge or a wool dauber. If you are using a sponge, make sure to rinse it out and squeeze it as dry as you can before starting. Any water left in the sponge will dilute your dye; this is okay if you want a more muted, lighter color, but if you are trying to achieve a saturated dark color, it will elongate the dyeing process as more layers will be required. The wool dauber does not need to be rinsed before use.

The process for applying alcohol- and water-based dyes begins much like the process for gel-based dyes. Apply dye to the back of your piece first, starting at the center and working your way out to the edges while rubbing in a circular motion. If you are working with a thin piece of leather (2–3 oz), be careful not to saturate the piece or the dye will bleed through to the front of your piece.

Once the back is covered, apply dye to the edges, adding more dye to your applicator as needed. Now you're ready to apply dye to the front. If you have paint on your piece, you can either go over it with the dye, which will change the color of the paint, or you can apply dye loosely around the painted areas and then use a paintbrush to fill in the details. If you choose to go over your paints with alcohol-based dyes, do so quickly and gently. The alcohol will dissolve the paint, and it will easily rub off if you work the surface too hard. Because alcohol- and water-based dyes applied over paint will

Apply dye loosely around the painted areas.

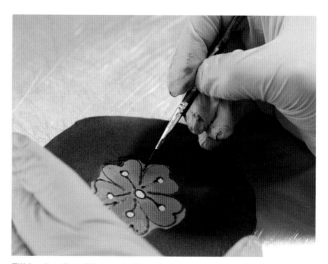

Fill in details with a paintbrush.

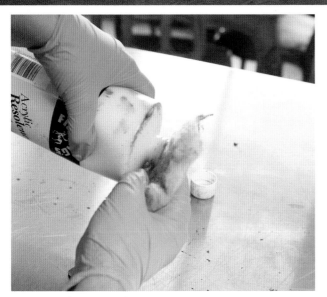

Pour a small amount of topcoat onto a sponge.

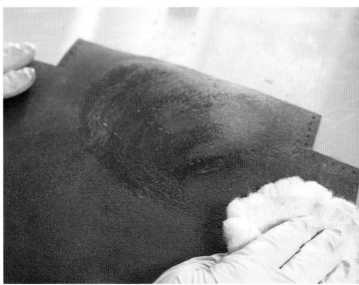

Apply a topcoat to the back side, rubbing in a circular motion.

dramatically change the colors, I recommend you test a sample first.

When you are done dyeing your piece, set it on your drying rack or a clean surface to dry. If you are dyeing more than one color, be sure to clean your work surface between colors.

PROTECTIVE TOPCOAT

After you have applied your paint and dye, it's time for a protective topcoat. The topcoat will protect your piece from some outside damage (such as water or coffee) and will also keep the dyes and paints that you just applied from bleeding or running off of your piece. To review the different types of topcoats available, see page 21.

Put your gloves on and apply your topcoat with a paper towel or a synthetic wool sponge. Place your dyed piece facedown on your work surface and pour a small amount of topcoat onto your sponge or a folded-up paper towel. Rub the topcoat on your piece in circular motions, making sure to cover the entire back, then pick up the piece and run the topcoat along the sides. Depending on the size of your piece, you may need to add more topcoat to your sponge or towel.

When you have finished the back and sides, add more topcoat to your sponge or towel and apply it to the front. Pay special attention to the painted areas; if you used gel (antique) stains, there may be some residual dye over the painted areas, and now is your chance to remove some of this. Just rub the topcoat in circular

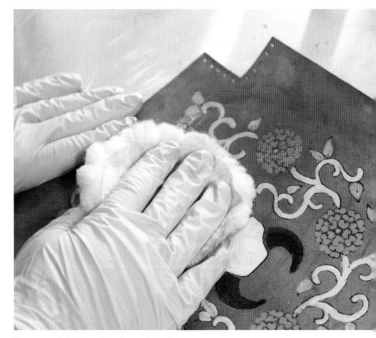

Pay special attention to painted areas.

motions over the entire piece, making sure you are working with a wet, but not soaked, applicator. If you rub hard with your topcoat on a piece that has antique stain, you will lift up any excess dye, which you may or may not want. Be careful not to leave visible drips or drops of topcoat on your piece; they will dry as sticky, raised globs.

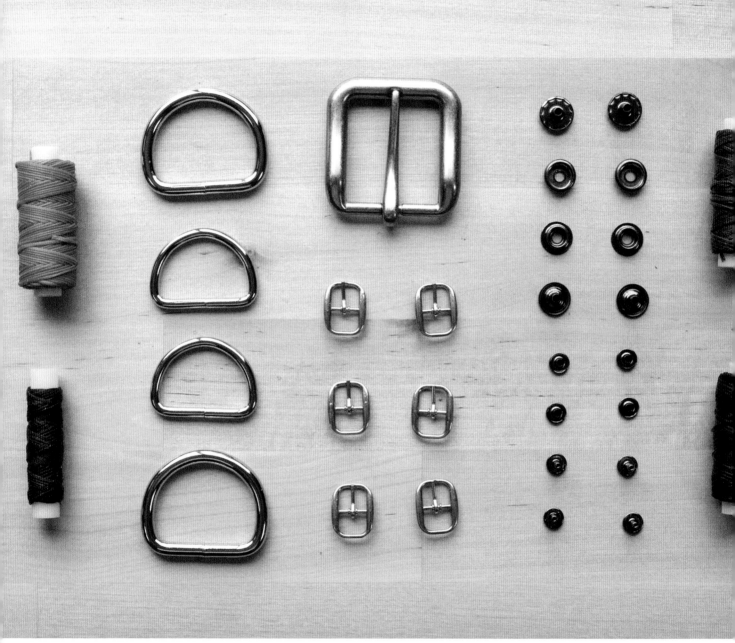

4

Assembly

After you have cut your patterns, added artwork, dyed and topcoated your pieces, adding hardware is usually the next step. In most cases, you will add the hardware to your piece prior to stitching since things such as snaps and rivets become more difficult to set once your piece is assembled.

When you're ready to assemble your piece into a three-dimensional, functional piece of leathercraft, you have a few options: One method uses rivets to attach leather pieces. Another option is to stitch your pieces together. A line of hand stitching is a little subtler than a line of rivets and can give a cleaner, more polished finish.

Attaching Hardware

RIVETS

Think of these like nailhead trim on furniture, except that a rivet is also a functional piece of hardware in your leathercraft. The rivet has two pieces: the post and the cap. The post is inserted into the bottom of the cap. Pressure applied by a hammer or rivet press to the rivet splays open the top of the post inside the cap so it does not come apart. Some rivets are called "locking cap" rivets, which means that once you have placed the cap onto the post piece it will stay in place. You still must set the rivet to secure it, but the locking cap keeps the rivet pieces together while you are preparing to set it, or placing other rivets.

There are many different sizes of rivets, both in cap size and post length. To determine the correct rivet for your project, look at the size of the post in comparison to the thickness of the leather you will rivet together. When you put the post part of the rivet through all of the layers of leather that you wish to rivet, the end of the post should stick up just far enough past the leather that you can put on the cap. Or, put another way, the rivet post should be just slightly longer than the thickness of the leathers that you wish to rivet together.

To set a rivet, first a punch hole in your leather at the spot where you would like it riveted together. You can use a relatively small punch for this, 3/32" (2.4mm) or so (size 1), since the rivet posts are generally pretty thin. Once your are holes punched, take the post end of your rivet and put it through a hole, then put the cap on. There are rivets that have a single cap and an unfinished back side, and there are rivets that are "double cap" that have a finished cap on both sides. If you are using the single cap rivet, be sure that the cap side is on the

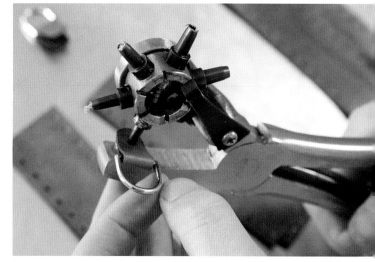

Punch a hole in the leather for the rivet.

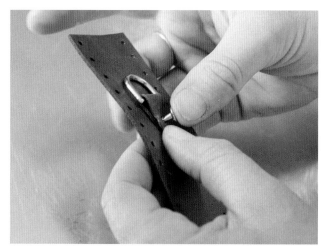

Put the post end of the rivet through the hole.

Put the cap on the post.

The two pieces of a rivet.

POST   **CAP**

outside of your piece so the finished portion shows when your piece is completed.

Once your rivet is in place, set it with your rivet setting tools. To do this with a hand setter, take your domed setting tool and your domed setting tray (see tools shown on page 22). Place the rivet in the smallest of the domes that it fits entirely in and, holding your leather in place, place the domed end of your setting tool on the top of the upward-facing rivet. Holding your setting tool at a 90-degree angle to the setting tray, hit your tool swiftly with your mallet. You may have to hit it several times to get the rivet to set.

If you are using a rivet press, choose the smallest die that the rivet will fit in entirely. A die that's too small will mark up the surface of your rivet, and one too large will leave an indented halo around the rivet. Once you have chosen your dies, put them in your rivet press. Place your leather piece with one cap of the rivet in the bottom tray and, holding it in place, press the handle firmly to set.

Once you have set your rivet, take your thumb and forefinger and put one on each side of the rivet to check if the caps are aligned. You can also hold up the side of the leather to view the two caps—are they aligned or have they gone off-kilter? If your rivet top and bottom are not aligned, your post was too long; the leather will keep the post in the proper place while you are setting the rivet, and if the rivet sticks out too far, the leather cannot hold the protruding portion in place. You will likely be able to cut off an improperly set rivet with pliers, but do so carefully to avoid ruining your piece.

Setting a rivet with the hand setter

Setting a rivet with the rivet press

RIVET TROUBLESHOOTING

A properly set rivet is flat against the surface of the leather, with no portions of the rivet higher or lower than the others. The caps are aligned on either side of the leather, rather than being offset. An offset rivet indicates a post that was too long, and a tilted rivet can indicate the same, or inconsistent pressure on the rivet while setting.

SNAPS

Snaps are set in a very similar way to rivets, but instead of having two parts, each snap has four. When you look at a snap where the pieces connect, there is a protruding piece on one end that fits into a hole on the other. The protruding piece is the "male" component of the snap and the hole is the "female" portion of the snap. Now, if you turn each of these snaps over and look at the opposite side, you will see the other piece of that portion of the snap, which is on the finished (decorative) side.

We will be using two types of snaps: Segma and Line 20 snaps. The Segma snaps look very much like a snap you would see on clothing. The Line 20 snaps, however, are slightly larger and are appropriate for other projects such as handbags and journals. If you are setting the snaps by hand, your snap and rivet setting kit will have all the tools you need.

For the Segma snaps, use the setter with a large bubble on the end to set the female portion. To set the female snap, put the small cap piece (the female decorative piece) cap-side down in the domed tray it fits best in. Press the female connective portion of the snap, the bowl-shaped piece, through the flesh side of the leather where you have punched your hole. Put your leather with the connective piece on top of the black cap, flesh side up, making sure it is aligned, and then place your tool at a 90-degree angle to the snap setting tray. Hit the end of your tool with a mallet to set the snap.

For the male portion, use the tool with the hole on the end. Place the male post side of the snap in the corresponding spot on the setting tray, then place your leather, grain side up, followed by the male connective piece (it looks a bit like a nipple). Place your tool again at a 90-degree angle to the rivet tray, and hit it with your mallet to set. Practice setting a few snaps before you put them on your pieces. A snap set too loosely will come apart with use.

To set the Line 20 snaps (and larger Line 24 if you choose to use them), use the tool with the small nipple on the end. To assemble a Line 20 snap, place the domed post piece of the snap (the post piece for the female portion) post-up in the corresponding-size dome on the snap setting tray. Place your leather on top of it (flesh side up), followed by the bowl-shaped connective portion of the female snap. Put the nipple on the tool straight into the hole on the post at a 90-degree angle,

Male Segma (left) and female Segma (right) snaps and rivet press dies

Male Line 20 (left) and female Line 20 (right) snaps and rivet press pieces

and then hit it with your mallet. You may have to hit it several times. This will curl the metal down so it creates a lip to keep the bowl-shaped portion in place. Use the same tool and method for the male side. Put the post part in the corresponding dome, followed by your leather (grain side up) and then the male portion of the snap. Again, place the tool in the hole at the top of the post and hit it with your mallet to set.

If you are setting your snaps using a hand press, you will choose the dies that fit each snap size and portion, such as the female portion for the Line 20, and place the

Female portion of the snap going through the leather

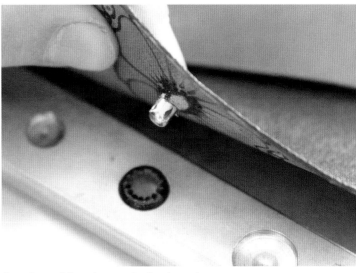

Cap piece of female snap in the domed tray

Setting the female snap portion with a hand setter

Setting the male snap portion with a rivet press

outer portion of your snap (the post side for the Line 20 snaps and the male Segma, or the cap for the female Segma snap) on the bottom tray, followed by your leather and then finally the connective portion of your snap. Press the handle to set. If you are unsure of the proper dies to use with your specific rivet press, do a test piece first. It is far better to waste one snap than all the time and energy you have just put into your project.

FOR A FINISHED LOOK ON BOTH SIDES

If you have a situation where both sides of a snap are exposed and you are using Line 20 or Line 24 snaps, you can use the more decorative post piece from the female portion in place of the male post portion on the male side of the piece. This will give your piece a finished look on both sides.

CLASPS

We will only be using clasps once in this book, but when you start to create your own patterns you will find them useful, especially when making bags. The clasps that we will use are called "turn-lock" or "twist-lock" clasps, and they have a little turning portion on a back piece that fits through a hole on the front portion of the clasp (say, on the flap of a bag). When you turn the back piece sideways, it prevents the front piece from moving, thus locking it in place.

The twist locks are four-piece assemblies, similar to snaps. They have a female portion, which is effectively a trim for the hole you will put on the bag flap, and a male portion that attaches to the bag body and goes through the female portion and twists to lock it in place. The female portion has a front and back piece; the male portion has the twisting piece that goes on the outside of the bag and a plate that goes on the inside to hold the outer piece in place.

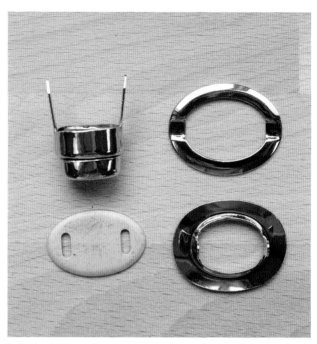

Twist-lock clasp pieces

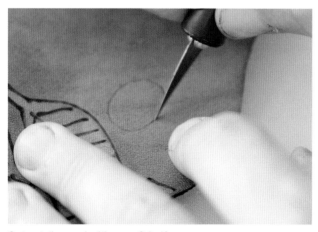

Decide where the clasp will go.

Draw an oval using the inside of the female piece.

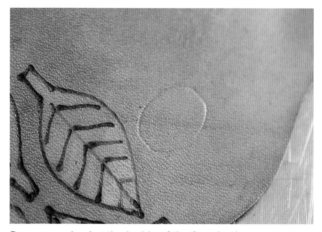

Cut out the oval with a craft knife.

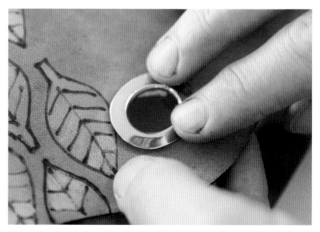

Stick the front female piece with the legs through the hole.

To install a twist-lock clasp, first cut a hole in the flap of your bag. Choose where you would like it to be, then use the back portion of the female piece (the one without the little legs) to draw the shape you will need to cut out (in this case, an oval). Draw your oval using the inside of this piece as your template, and then cut it carefully with a craft knife or leather knife.

To install the female piece, place the front female piece on the top of the bag with the legs sticking through the holes that you just cut out. You may need to trim some of the leather with your knife so it fits without leather protruding into the hole. It is always better to start with a hole that is too small if you are unsure of the size; you can make the hole bigger much more easily than you can make it smaller.

After the front flap piece is in place, fit the back piece on the underside of the flap, divot side up. Gently press the legs away from the hole with your fingers to keep it in place, then use pliers to pull them away from the hole and the rest of the way down. Press the legs further with the pliers; just be sure to put a piece of scrap leather between the front piece and the bottom of your pliers so you don't mark the pieces with your pliers.

To attach the male side, take the twisting piece of the closure. Close your bag, making sure it aligns the way you would like it to along the edges, and that you have left as much space as you would like between the sides and the fold of the flap. Then, put the legs of the twisting piece through the flap piece you just installed and press. This will create a mark on the bag where the two legs go. Take your knife and make two small slits, no larger than the size of the legs, on the front of the bag. Push the legs through the slits and put the male backing piece on the legs on the inside of the bag. Take your pliers and bend the legs toward one another as best you can.

Use pliers to pull the legs of the clasp.

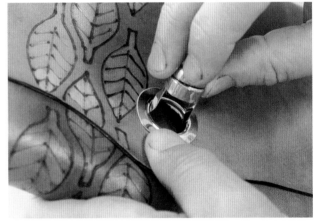

Push the twisting piece through the flap to mark placement.

Make small slits for the legs.

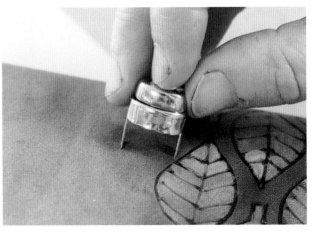

Push the legs through the slits.

BUCKLES

To attach a buckle, you will want to split a piece of strap on the end to reduce its thickness for ease of folding (see page 16 for splitting tools and instructions). How far in you split the strap will depend on the type and size of the buckle you are using and on the width of your strap. You can estimate by folding the leather over and looking at it in conjunction with the buckle. You will need enough space for the leather to go around the bar and then to rivet it at the end. For a 1½" (3.8cm) strap, you will split approximately 3" (7.6cm) on the end of the strap.

After you have split it, mark the center of the split on the grain side. This will be ¾" (1.9cm) from either edge and 1½" (3.8cm) from the end of the strap. Make two additional marks ¼" (6mm) from the first mark along the length of the strap in either direction, also centered. Punch these with a size 1 (³⁄₃₂" [2.4mm]) punch, then use your knife to connect the sides of the circles to create a slot. Put the slot over the bar on your buckle and wrap it around the back.

Check that the tongue can move freely. If your slot needs to be longer or wider, alter it as needed using your punch and knife. Once you have a slot appropriately sized, mark a hole for the rivet to hold the buckle in place. Mark it approximately ½" (1.3cm) from the end of your slot, centered on the strap. Punch the hole, then fold the piece and mark the corresponding hole in the other side of the leather. Be sure that the slot is centered on the fold when you do this. Punch the second hole and add the rivet (see pages 50–51).

Slot for tongue

Put the bar through the slot and wrap the belt around.

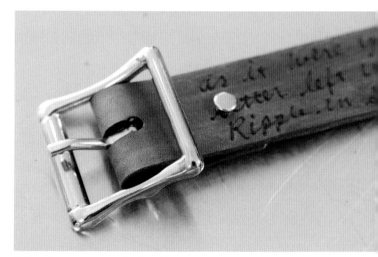

Add a rivet to secure the buckle.

Stitching

In this book, we will use hand stitching rather than machine stitching, and there are several reasons for this. One is that it is very durable. By individually prepunching the holes in your leathercraft project you can use thicker thread than a machine would allow. This will minimize breakage and lessen the chances that your piece will need to be restitched down the road. Additionally, leather is not self-healing, so once you put a hole in it, whether by machine needle, pin or anything else, the hole will always be there. If you were to sew with a machine and your stitches came out, you would need to restitch using the same tiny holes. Hand punching at least gives you a larger hole to restitch, should you ever need to repair the stitches on your piece.

My favorite reason for learning hand stitching is that it requires a very minimal investment, and it is easier to learn than machine sewing. You already have the tools you need to punch the holes (a rotary punch or a drive punch and mallet); all you need is a needle and thread—and, of course, your hands.

SETTING UP YOUR STITCHING

Before you start stitching, be sure that your leather piece is completely dry and the stitching holes are punched with a size 00 punch (1/16" [1.6mm]). A wet piece of leather can stretch and distort during stitching, and also any residual dye and topcoat left in your prepunched holes will deposit on your hands (which is fine if you're in a rush and need to stitch something, you'll just be a bit messier than you would otherwise). Be sure that your stitching area is free of small debris and hairs. Pet hairs tend to stick very well to a waxed thread, which will result in a number of hairs stuck in the holes and stitches of your final piece. Small bits of leather, other dust and fuzz will all do the same.

Once you have a clean work space, look carefully at your piece. When you stitch vegetable-tanned leather you will not be turning your piece inside out to stitch, but rather doing it with the right sides out as you make your stitches. Sew any interior portions such as pockets and silicone cases first, then move on to the outer seams. Building your piece this way allows you better access to the interior portions and makes some of the constructions that we will later learn possible.

Stitching details

One thing to consider, especially on smaller items such as a wallet or a cell phone case, is where you would like your stitches to end. At the end of your stitches you will lock them to keep them from unraveling, and in doing so will build up a little extra bulk. While not totally offensive, you may prefer to keep it on the back of your piece. If this is the case, begin stitching where you want your stitches to end.

STARTING TO STITCH

To start your stitching, first measure and cut a piece of thread. If you're sewing a straight stitch, you will want to cut roughly 2¼ times the length that you need to stitch. For example, when I cut thread to stitch a wallet, I make two large loops around the wallet with the thread to estimate my needed length. It is a rough estimate, but it generally works.

Next, thread the needle. If you are stitching a long seam, secure your thread in place. To do this, take the short tail end of the thread and open up a small hole in it. Pull your needle through this hole, then pull on the long tail to "lock" your needle. When you are done stitching you will need to cut your needle free, but it's worth it. With a locked needle the thread will not slip out as you are stitching.

After you have threaded your needle and chosen your starting point, it's time to start stitching. Pull half of your thread through the first stitch (you'll use the second half of the thread later). To stitch a standard running stitch, bring the needle up through one hole and down through the next until you come back to your starting point. Each stitch should be pulled tight to the leather, but not so tight that you are putting stress or

COBBLER'S STITCH
. . . .

If you're stitching a piece that will be difficult to access once you have stitched the first line of running stitch, you can do something called a "cobbler's" or "saddle" stitch. For this, put one needle on each end of your long thread and start at the most difficult place to access. With your needles on opposite sides of your piece, stitch using two running stitches simultaneously.

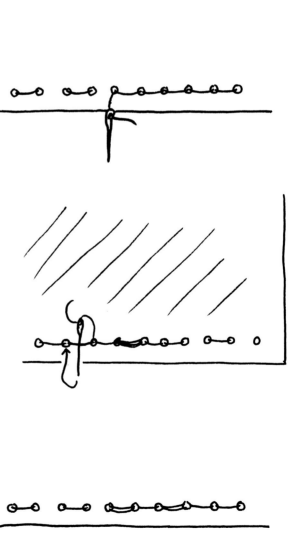

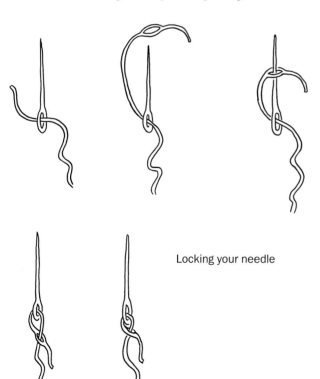

Locking your needle

Locking your stitch

Trim the thread after locking the stitches.

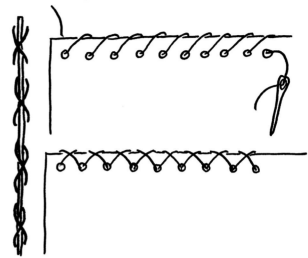

Wrap the stitches around the edges, creating *x*'s.

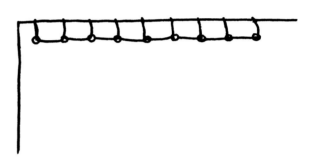

Modified blanket stitch in every hole

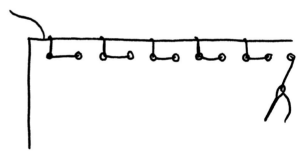

Modified banket stitch in every other hole

strain on the piece itself. To test proper stitch tension, take your fingernail and "pluck" the stitch as you would a guitar string. If it makes a sound, your stitch has proper tension. If it moves much, your stitch is too loose. If it doesn't move and doesn't make a sound, your stitch is too tight.

Stitch all the way around your piece with a running stitch, then lock your stitches in place. To do this, reverse your stitch direction for three stitches, then go forward again for two, ending on the inside of your piece. Wrap your thread around a stitch, and then put it through the next hole. Cut the thread close to the piece. Backstitching will keep your stitches in place, and the risk of stitches coming undone is substantially less than with a knot. It looks better, too.

After you have stitched once around the piece, thread your needle on the long tail you left behind. Stitching in the opposite direction, continue with your running stitch so you form a solid line of stitching. When you have completed your stitching, lock your stitches again with this end of the thread and clip the excess.

OTHER STITCHING STYLES

You can certainly experiment with styles of stitching other than a standard running stitch. If you are constructing a piece that has wrong sides together with the stitch line close to the edge, you can take your thread at every hole, or every other hole, and wrap it around the side of the piece before moving on to the next hole. This is what I refer to as a modified blanket stitch.

Or, you can wrap each stitch around the edge, coming up from the bottom of your piece each time. The end result of this style is to create a series of *x*'s along the edge of the piece. The difficulty with this style is that you cannot lock your stitches. You must tie a knot, preferably inside your piece, to secure your thread. Before you do, it is helpful to wrap the stitch around the edge a few times to secure it.

ADHESIVES AND STITCHING

There are many different types of glue that you can use for leather with different purposes. For a discussion on the different types of adhesives, see page 24.

Many leatherworkers will tell you that the proper way to hand stitch your items is first to glue your pieces together where you are going to stitch them, then punch the holes, and finally to stitch. I have employed this technique on and off over the years. Yes, it certainly saves you from punching the holes twice, but there are a few drawbacks. One is that the glues used for this are never quite permanent, and they never quite adhere themselves only to the inside of your piece. This means you're often left with a sticky edge between the seam and the end of the leather.

The second problem is that when you are using a rotary or drive punch, your punches have an "entry" and "exit" hole. They look different, and the exit hole is not quite as clean as the entry. If you prepunch your holes with your rotary or drive punch, punching from the grain side to the flesh side, the entry holes will be on the outside of your piece (since you will stitch with wrong sides together). If you glue first, your entry holes will be on the outside, and the exit holes on the inside of your piece. It is certainly acceptable, but you may decide you don't like the look any more than I do.

Additionally, I'd much rather punch a hole in the wrong spot on a piece that I have just cut, rather than one that I have already put artwork on and am ready to stitch.

All these things aside, if you are using your adhesive to help with the stitching process, you will want to apply a light layer of your glue to each of the pieces you are stitching together. Apply it as you would a coat of paint: evenly, thinly, with no globs. Apply it just to the line where your seam will be, and make sure it is on the parts that will be in contact when your piece is finished. In other words, if you are stitching wrong-sides together, apply your adhesive to the wrong (flesh) sides of your piece. If you are stitching two pieces that overlap, apply the glue to the wrong (flesh) side of the top piece and the right (grain) side of the bottom piece.

Allow your glue to dry to a light tack before carefully aligning and pressing the two pieces together. If you are using contact cement it will stick immediately and the bond will harden over time. If you need to reposition it, do so before you press the pieces together because they will very quickly get harder to separate.

Once your pieces are glued, you can then punch your holes. Punch from the front of your piece, whenever possible, using a piece of scrap as a backing sheet if you are using a rotary punch (this encourages clean exit holes). After you have punched all of your holes, stitch as you normally would.

Entry holes on left, exit holes on right

STITCHING PRACTICE

Using our two practice pieces from the end of Chapter 2, it is time to try out the techniques we just discussed.

1 Look at the pieces and how they fit together. Decide where you would like your stitches to end.

2 Estimate your thread length and cut your thread. If you are going to be doing something other than a straight running stitch (which requires only 2¼–2½ times the length that you need to stitch), you may need more thread. Thread your needle and lock it (optional).

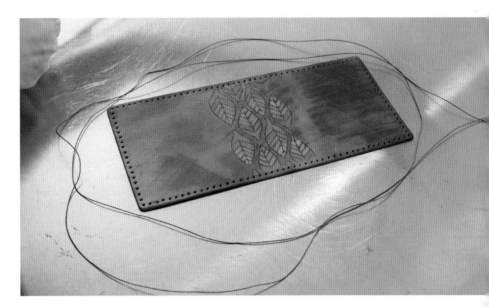

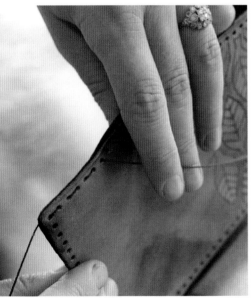

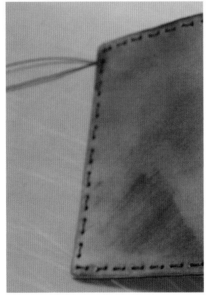

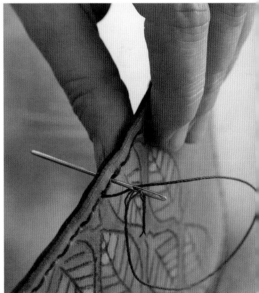

3 Start stitching. Pull your thread halfway through the starting hole and stitch once around the piece using a running stitch.

4 When you have stitched through each hole once, lock your stitches and cut your thread close to your piece.

5 Thread your needle through the remaining half of your thread and stitch in the opposite direction around your piece, filling in the gaps so there is a solid line of stitching. When finished, lock your stitches and clip the excess thread.

Projects

Now that we've reviewed the tools and techniques you need to create your own leatherwork, it's time to get started on the projects. The projects in this section are arranged according to difficulty. We start with a rather simple keychain that will get you comfortable working with leather, and build from there, ending with a gorgeous messenger bag. It isn't necessary to work your way through the projects in the order in which they appear, but be aware that the later projects are more difficult.

I do provide patterns for many of the projects, but also give you tips on how to create your own patterns. For example, the keychain lends itself well to many different shapes. Feel free to experiment beyond the basic circle shape shown in the steps. When it comes time to decorate your pieces, feel free to use my designs as inspiration, but I encourage you to create your own. That is what will make your piece unique. I show a variety of decorative patterns on the finished projects so you can see how endless the options are for design. If you're not yet confident in your decorating skills, look to illustration books for help. When I first started, I relied on Celtic and Art Nouveau design books to help with the decoration. I've since developed my own style and urge you to find your own style as well.

KEYCHAIN

MATERIALS

4-5 oz or 5-6 oz leather

Template (page 124) (optional)

Key ring

Cardstock and sharp paper scissors

Rivet

Hand rivet setter (and mallet) or press

Marking and cutting tools (pages 14–16)

Punching tools (page 17), including size 1 (³⁄₃₂" [2.4mm]) drive or rotary punch

Decorative pattern tools (page 18)

Painting and dyeing supplies (pages 19-21), including neatsfoot oil

For our first project we are going to create something functional that you will use every day: a keychain. You can use the pattern provided, or if you would like to create your own custom shape, you can certainly do that as well. See the sidebar below for tips on creating your own custom pattern. Because it will see a lot of use and you will want it to hold its shape, choose a relatively thick piece of leather.

TECHNIQUE REVIEW

- ► Preparing and Tracing Your Pattern (page 32)
- ► Cutting Out Your Pattern (page 33)
- ► Branding Leather (pages 38–39)
- ► Carving Leather (pages 40–41)
- ► Adding Color (pages 42–47)
- ► Attaching Hardware (pages 50–51)

TO CREATE YOUR OWN PATTERN

The pattern shown in the steps is a simple round keychain that will rivet to the ring, but if you are creating your own pattern you can cut whatever shape you would like. Because it is your first project, you might want to keep the shape simple. This is a relatively quick project, so you can always make another more complicated version later.

To make your own pattern, either sketch it first or just draw it right onto your pattern paper. First, draw a tab that will fold over the key ring and rivet. To draw this tab, make a rectangle that is 2" (5.1cm) long and at least ¾" (1.9cm) wide. Mark two holes centered in the width of the rectangle and ⅜" (1cm) in from either end. These will be your rivet holes.

Once you have the tab in place, draw your keychain shape off the end of one short side of the rectangle. Feel free to change the shape of the rectangle, varying the width, making it curved or shaping it in any way you want. Just remember that you will have to cut it out.

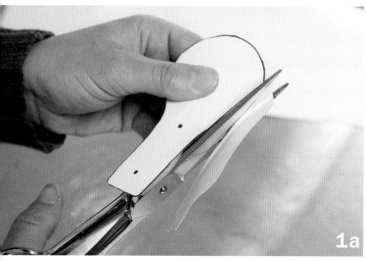 

1 CREATE YOUR PATTERN

From the cardstock, cut out your pattern (either the pattern provided or the pattern you created), and punch the two holes using a size 1 punch.

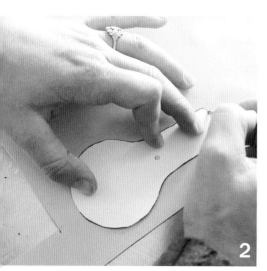 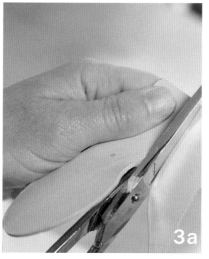 

2 TRACE YOUR PATTERN

Trace around your pattern on the grain side of the leather, making sure to mark the holes.

3 CUT OUT THE SHAPE

Cut the leather and punch the holes using a drive or rotary punch. Fold over the top of the leather to make sure your holes align.

CUTTING SMALL SHAPES

When you are cutting out a small shape, especially out of thick leather, it may be easier for you to cut if you "choke up" on your scissors, cutting with the section of the scissors closest to your hand, rather than cutting with the tip. You have less leverage and therefore less strength with the tip of the scissors, and because it is the farthest from your hand, you also have less control.

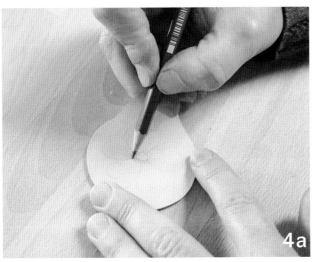

4 ADD YOUR DECORATIVE DESIGN

Practice your design on paper first or sketch it directly onto your keychain using a pencil (a 4B or a 5B will work best).

The thickness of the leather means it is appropriate for carving, but the size might be difficult since you need a good hold on your piece to carve it. If you are feeling ambitious and would like to carve it, wetting the leather lightly with a sponge will help the carving gouge move through it more smoothly.

For this example, I branded my pattern. Make sure your branding iron is hot, and hold the keychain with your support hand as far away from the branding iron as possible.

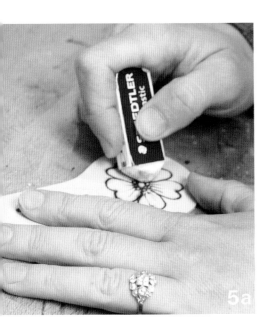

5 ADD COLOR TO YOUR DESIGN

Once your pattern outline is complete, erase any visible pencil lines. You are now ready to paint your design. Dip your wool dauber in rubbing alcohol and rub the entire grain surface of the leather with rubbing alcohol before you begin. This opens the pores of the leather and helps the paint adhere better.

Remember to paint your piece in thin, even layers; let your paint dry completely before moving on to the next step.

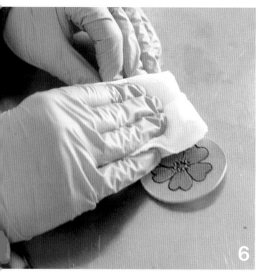

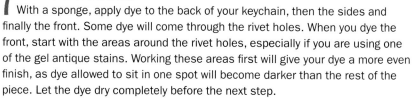

6 OIL YOUR PIECE

Once the paint is completely dry, oil your piece. Pour a bit of neatsfoot oil onto a paper towel and rub the oil into the grain side of your leather.

7 DYE THE LEATHER

With a sponge, apply dye to the back of your keychain, then the sides and finally the front. Some dye will come through the rivet holes. When you dye the front, start with the areas around the rivet holes, especially if you are using one of the gel antique stains. Working these areas first will give your dye a more even finish, as dye allowed to sit in one spot will become darker than the rest of the piece. Let the dye dry completely before the next step.

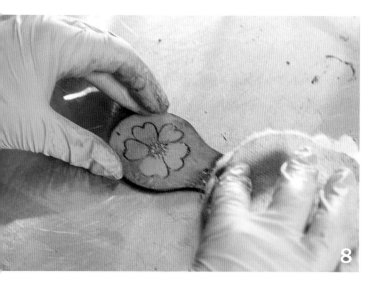

8 APPLY THE TOPCOAT

Once the dye is dry, examine for any light spots, touching them up with more dye as needed, then apply the topcoat. Add a little topcoat to your sponge or paper towel. Starting on the back of your piece, apply the topcoat in a circular motion until you have covered the entire back, then the sides and front.

The topcoat does not need to be worked in; a correctly applied topcoat should appear slightly filmy and white when you are applying it, then disappear almost immediately. Even out obvious spots of topcoat before the topcoat dries. Once the piece has been covered, put it onto a rack to dry.

DYE TOO DARK?

When using the gel antique stains there is a range of how the dyes will appear on the leather. If your dye is too dark, you've likely put too much on your sponge or paper towel when you were applying it. The dye can't be removed once it is there, so the best thing to do is to try some new techniques the next time around. If your dye is too dark, the next time you dye try working with a slightly damp sponge (not sopping wet, just damp). You can also try applying new dye to the back of the piece only, then using the dye that is in your sponge for the front. Add dye a little at a time, working it into the leather as you go. This should give you a lighter finish. That said, different pieces of leather absorb and resist dye differently, so some will be darker than others no matter what you do.

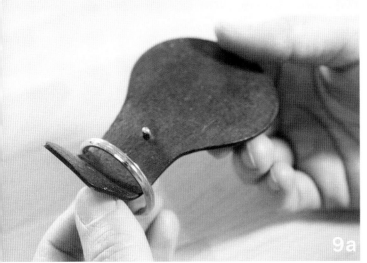

9a 9b

9 ASSEMBLE THE KEYCHAIN

Put the post piece of the rivet through the leather on the grain side of the keychain so the post is visible on the flesh side. Put the leather through the key ring and wrap it around, pushing the post of the rivet through the other rivet hole. Take the cap of the rivet and snap it on so that the leather stays looped around the key ring.

10 SET THE RIVET

Use either your press or a mallet and hand rivet setter to set your rivet down about halfway. Look at it from the side and check to make sure that the top and bottom cap are still aligned. If they are not aligned, the rivet is too long. You can either pull it apart or cut it off with a pair of pliers and try again with a rivet with a shorter post.

If the caps are aligned, go ahead and set it completely. Press it hard; it is the only thing holding your keychain together!

10a

11 FINISHING TOUCH-UPS

Once your keychain is riveted together, check your piece for any spots that the dye has missed. If any of your pattern is on the curved part of the leather, check to see if the branding or carving lines have cracked. If so, touch them up with a little dye. To do this, apply a small amount of dye to a paper towel or your sponge and rub it on the area needing to be touched up. Gel dyes won't penetrate your topcoat, but the alcohol- and water-based dyes will, so these should be applied carefully. Use another small piece of paper towel to apply some topcoat to the touched-up area.

Put your keys on it, and enjoy your first finished leather project!

10b

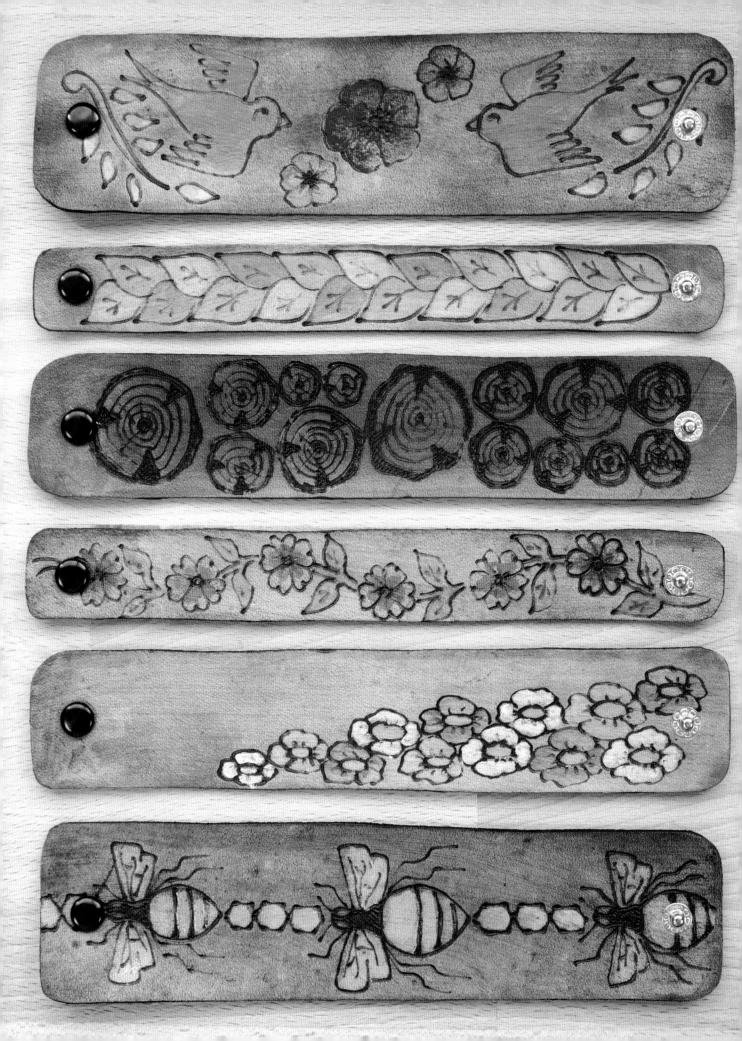

CUFF

MATERIALS

3-4 oz leather

Cardstock and sharp paper scissors

For fixed-length cuff: Segma snap, hand snap setter (and mallet) or press

For adjustable cuff: center-bar buckle, rivet, hand rivet setter (and mallet) or press

Marking and cutting tools (pages 14-16), including cloth tape measure

Punching tools (page 17), including size 1 (3/32" [2.4mm]) drive or rotary punch, and smallest punch you have

Decorative pattern tools (page 18)

Painting and dyeing supplies (pages 19-21)

A cuff can vary from something very basic to an embellished piece of wearable art. How complex and how decorated you would like your cuff to be is entirely up to you. This project will cover the basics, and your imagination can do the rest. Your leather should be thick enough to be durable and hold its shape, but flexible enough that it will be comfortable and can make the turn around the buckle for the adjustable cuff.

TECHNIQUE REVIEW

- ▶ Preparing and Tracing Your Pattern (page 32)
- ▶ Cutting Out Your Pattern (page 33)
- ▶ Branding Leather (pages 38–39)
- ▶ Carving Leather (pages 40–41)
- ▶ Adding Color (pages 42–47)
- ▶ Attaching Hardware (pages 50–53, 56)

ADJUSTABLE OR FIXED CUFF?

The first thing you will need to decide about your cuff is whether you want it to be a fixed length or if you would prefer an adjustable closure. If you are making one for yourself or for someone whose wrist you can measure, a fixed-length cuff is a great choice. If you are making one for someone whose wrist size you know only approximately, or whose wrist may still be growing, an adjustable cuff is best.

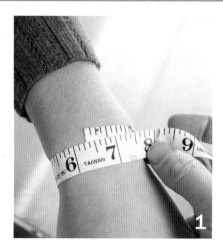

1 DETERMINE YOUR MEASUREMENTS

Measure your wrist, or the wrist that the cuff should eventually fit. To do this, take a cloth tape measure and wrap it around your wrist at the bone. Pull it so there is no slack in the tape measure, but not so tight that it feels snug. Write down the measurement.

Decide the width of your cuff: Usually cuffs are between 1"–2" (2.5cm–5.1cm) wide, but you can certainly make yours whatever width you choose. For this project it is best to stay between ¾" (1.9cm) and 3" (7.6cm).

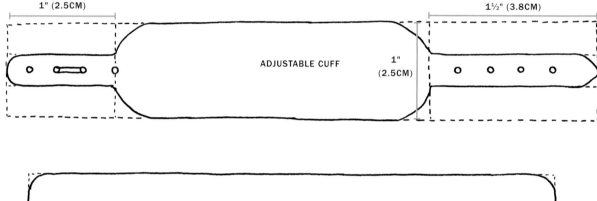

1" (2.5CM) ADJUSTABLE CUFF 1" (2.5CM) 1½" (3.8CM)

FIXED-LENGTH CUFF

2 DRAW YOUR PATTERN

For an adjustable cuff: On your cardstock, draw a rectangle the width you would like your cuff to be and 1" (2.5cm) shorter than your wrist measurement.

Find the center of the short edge of each side of your rectangle. Measure ¼" (6mm) in either direction toward the edges and mark the locations with your pencil. From these marks, draw 1" (2.5cm) lines outside the rectangle on one side, and 1½" (3.8cm) lines on the other side. This creates the buckle tab and the adjustment tab on your cuff. Draw a rounded end on the 1" (2.5cm) tab and a pointed end on the 1½" (3.8cm) tab.

Mark four adjustment holes ¼" (6mm) apart on the long tab, starting ¼" (6mm) from where the tab meets the cuff. On the short tab, mark a hole where the tab meets the cuff, then three more holes each ¼" (6mm) apart.

For a fixed-length cuff: On your cardstock, draw a rectangle the width you want your cuff to be and the length 1½" (3.8cm) longer than your wrist measurement. Mark two centered holes ⅜" (1cm) in from each end. These will be the holes for your snaps.

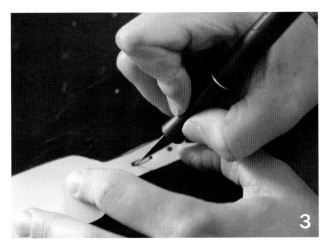

3 CUT OUT YOUR PATTERN

Using sharp paper scissors, cut carefully along the edges of your pattern. Using a rotary or drive punch, punch the holes where marked. These are just guide holes so you know where to mark holes on your leather; use the smallest size punch you have.

On the short tab of the adjustable cuff, punch the two center holes with a size 1 punch, then connect the outer edges of the holes using your craft knife to create a slot for your buckle tongue.

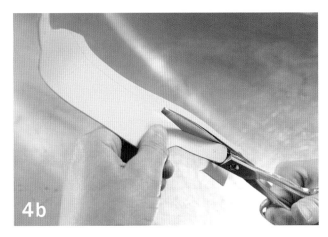

4 CUT THE PATTERN OUT OF LEATHER

Lay the pattern on your piece of leather and trace around it. Cut the leather and punch holes where indicated with a size 1 punch. If you are making an adjustable cuff, cut the slot just as you did in the pattern.

5 SKETCH YOUR DESIGN

Draw your decorative design onto the leather with a pencil. Sketch out any elements you would like to brand or carve.

6 BRAND OR CARVE YOUR DESIGN

Depending on your design, either brand the design into the leather or carve away sections of the leather to reveal the design. In this example, I've written on my cuff and will brand the words into the leather.

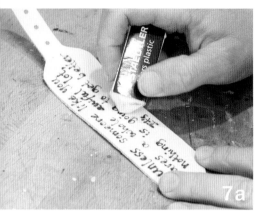
7a

7b

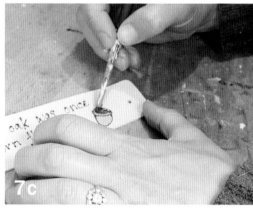
7c

7 ADD COLOR

Erase any remaining sketch marks with your eraser. Use a wool dauber to apply rubbing alcohol on the piece. Apply paint anywhere you would like, remembering to apply it thinly, layering if needed, to prevent globs.

CREATIVE CUTS

Some ideas to give your cuff a unique twist: Try cutting out the negative space (the background or space between objects) in your pattern to give it a leather "lace" feel. Or, go the opposite direction and create a few little cutout leather pieces that you can rivet on, such as flowers, leaves or little bugs.

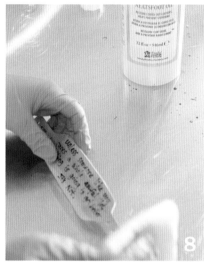
8

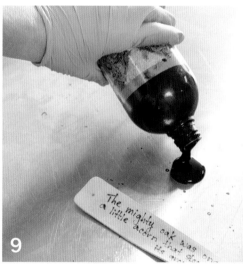
9

8 APPLY OIL

Once the paint is completely dry, apply neatsfoot oil using a paper towel or synthetic wool.

9 DYE THE LEATHER

Choose your dye color and apply it. Because this piece has holes, dye the back quickly, saving the spots around the holes for last. Then dye the sides and the spaces around the holes on the front first, followed by the remainder of the front.

10

10 APPLY THE TOPCOAT

Once the dye dries, apply the topcoat. Be sure to coat the entire piece without leaving any globs of topcoat on your piece. Set the cuff aside to dry.

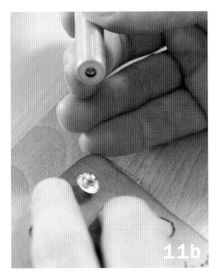

11 ASSEMBLE YOUR CUFF: FIXED LENGTH

For the fixed-length cuff, use Segma snaps. Take out all the snap pieces and put the male parts together and the female parts together. Starting with the male parts, put the male post through the cuff so the flat piece is on the back side (flesh side) of your cuff and the post is visible on the front (grain side).

Put the male connector piece on and either set with a hand snap setter or with your press. Take the connecting portion of the female side and push it through the leather on the other side of your cuff from the flesh side; the top of the dome will come through onto the grain side and you will see the concave hole on the flesh side. Place the black cap for the female side on top of the protruding piece on the grain side. Set using your snap setter.

12 ASSEMBLE YOUR CUFF: ADJUSTABLE LENGTH

For the adjustable-length cuff, you only need to set one rivet. Since your slot is already cut, take a ½" (1.3cm) center-bar buckle and thread the small tab through it, then fold the tab around the bar so the two holes meet. Place a rivet through the holes and press with a rivet setter.

BELT

MATERIALS

Leather strap in desired width

Marking and cutting tools, including cloth tape measure and splitter (pages 14–16)

Decorative pattern tools (page 18)

Painting and dyeing supplies (pages 19–21)

For permanent buckle: center- or heel-bar buckle; rivet; rivet hand setter (and mallet) or press; punching tools (page 17), including size 2 ($\frac{1}{8}$" [3.2mm]), size 1 ($\frac{3}{32}$" [2.4mm]) (for rivets) and size 0 ($\frac{5}{64}$" [2mm]) drive or rotary punches, punch sized for holes that fit your buckle tongue, and end punch (optional)

For removable buckle: trophy-style buckle; Segma snap; hand snap setter (and mallet) or press; punching tools (page 17), including size 1 ($\frac{3}{32}$" [2.4mm]) drive or rotary punch, and punch sized for holes that fit the "male" piece on your buckle

Cuffs are fun, but not quite big enough to really show off. Well, how about a belt? A belt is something near and dear to my heart because belts were how I got my start in leatherworking. And once you've made yourself a vegetable-tanned leather belt you will wonder why anyone would wear anything else.

You could start your belt with a precut and prepunched belt strap. Tandy sells them, and while they work perfectly, they don't offer you all of the options that you get by starting from scratch—or at least by starting halfway from scratch. For this project we will start with a leather strap rather than a full leather hide.

TECHNIQUE REVIEW

- ▶ Branding Leather (pages 38–39)
- ▶ Carving Leather (pages 40–41)
- ▶ Adding Color (pages 42–47)
- ▶ Attaching Hardware (pages 50–53, 56)

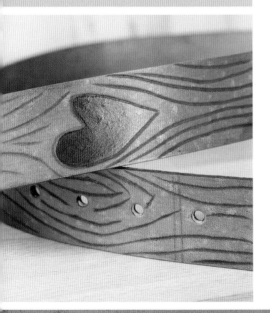

1 DETERMINE THE BELT SIZE

Decide how wide you would like your belt to be. Most jeans have loops that will fit belts up to 1¾" (4.4cm) wide, so if you are planning on wearing your belt with jeans, something that wide or narrower is ideal. If you will be wearing the belt on an outfit without belt loops (over a dress, for example), you could go all the way up to 2½" (6.4cm), or down to ½" (1.3cm). Once you've decided on your belt width, purchase a leather strap with that dimension.

Next, decide how long to make your belt. If you have a belt that fits you well, measure it from the end of the leather (where it folds over at the buckle end) to the hole that you use most. You can also wrap a cloth tape measure around your waist to get a usable measurement.

2 CHOOSE A BELT STYLE

Now decide what type of buckle you will be using with your strap. With a center- or heel-bar buckle, you need a slot for the buckle tongue to pass through. If you are using a trophy style, you do not need a slot. We will cover the center/heel-bar style but know you can omit this if you are using a trophy style.

3 SPLIT THE BUCKLE END OF THE BELT

Splitting the leather first allows it to fold more neatly over the buckle. Mark 4" (10.2cm) in from the end on the flesh side of the strap if you are using a center/heel-bar buckle or 3" (7.6cm) in for a trophy style. This is how far in you will split the leather. You can use a hand splitter or you can use a roll type. If you have a hand splitter, hold it at a slight angle to the leather on the flesh side and draw it toward you. Vary the angle to change the cutting depth, but be aware that too steep an angle will make it difficult to cut. Repeat this process until the leather is split to half its original thickness. For a roll splitter, clamp the leather between the drum and the blade, flesh side up, and lock it in place using the handle, then pull.

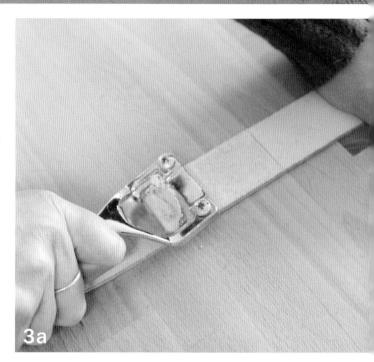

3a

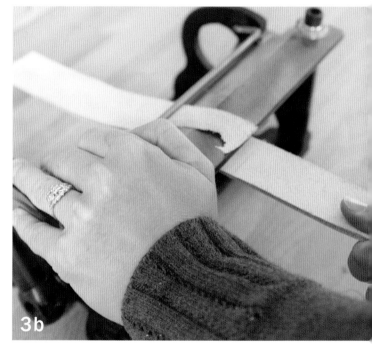

3b

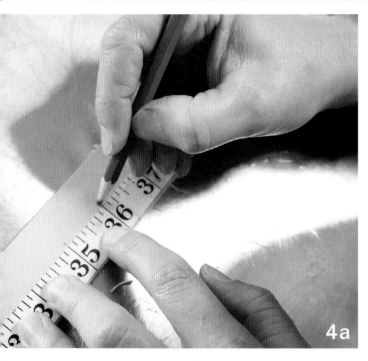

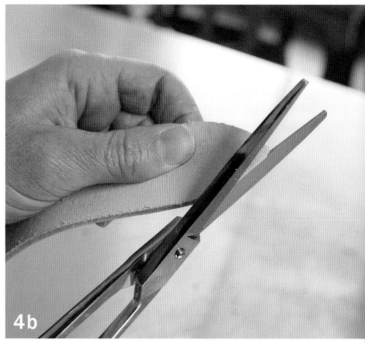

4 MARK THE ADJUSTMENT HOLES

Add 8" (20.3cm) to your waist measurement for a trophy style or 10" (25.4cm) for a heel- or center-bar style. Measuring from the split end, mark this distance along the center of the belt strap; this marks the other end of your belt. Working backwards from this mark, mark a hole 5" (12.7cm) in from the end mark and then six additional holes spaced 1" (2.5cm) apart.

Cut the leather at the end mark using either an end punch or your scissors (if you are using your scissors, you may wish to shape the end into a point). Punch the seven holes using a drive or rotary punch; the size of punch you use will depend on the type of buckle you have, so do some comparing of your buckle tongue (or hook on the trophy style) to the punches to find which one will work best (you can always make the holes bigger later).

4c

1" (2.5CM)   5" (12.7CM)   END MARK

5 MARK FOR THE BUCKLE

For the trophy style: On the split end of the belt, mark centered holes at ⅜" (9.5mm), ⅞" (2.2cm), 2⅛" (5.5cm) and 2⅝" (6.7cm). Punch these with a size 1 punch.

For the bar-style buckle: On the split end, mark centered holes at ⅜" (1cm), 1" (2.5cm), 1⅝" (4.1cm), 2⅜" (6cm), 3" (7.6cm) and 3⅝" (9.2cm) from the end. The outer two holes on each end of the belt will be snap holes, and the two center holes will create the slot for the buckle tongue. Punch the outer holes with a size 1 punch and the inner holes with a size 2. Connect the ends of the size 2 punch holes using your knife to create a slot.

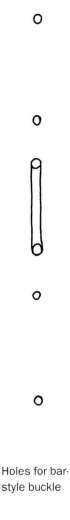

Holes for bar-style buckle

6 ADD A DECORATIVE PATTERN

Sketch your design first, if needed, and then brand and carve. I recommend carving for belts; you are using a thicker leather well-suited to carving, and the carving lasts longer than the branding does when exposed to the kind of use a belt will get.

7 ADD COLOR
Erase any pencil marks and apply rubbing alcohol to help the paint adhere. Apply the paint in thin layers.

8 ADD OIL, DYE AND APPLY THE TOPCOAT
Once the paint is dry, oil your belt, dye it and apply the topcoat, paying attention to the dye coming through the holes (refer to step 9 of the cuff project).

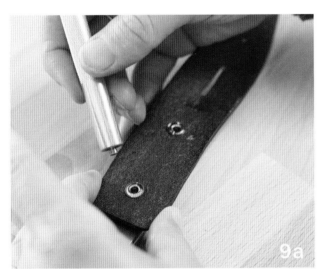

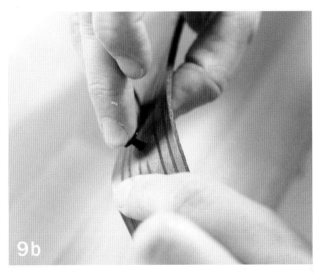

9 ASSEMBLE THE BELT
After the topcoat has dried, it is time to assemble your belt (both trophy style and bar style are assembled the same way). Choose whether you want to use rivets or snaps on your belt: Use snaps if you'd like a removable buckle. If you are using snaps, the smaller Segma snaps work best for the belts as they sit flatter than the Line 20 or 24. Apply the snaps or rivets. If using snaps, the connective portions will face inward (visible on the flesh side of the leather). Use female ends for the two holes at the far end and male ends for the snaps that will be visible when the belt is worn.

TO MAKE A STAY

If you find your belt tail flopping around, you might want to make a little stay. To do this, cut a piece of scrap leather (using 4–5 oz if available) that is about ½" (1.3cm) wide and long enough to wrap loosely around your belt strap. Punch one size 00 (1⁄16" [1.6mm]) hole in each end. Dye the stay to match your belt and use your needle and thread to stitch the stay together using the holes you punched. Thread the stay on your belt and position it between the sets of snaps on your belt.

CATCHALL TRAY

MATERIALS

4-5 oz or 5-6 oz leather

Marking and cutting tools (pages 14-16), including carpenter's square

Punching tools (page 17), including size 00 (1⁄16" [1.6mm]) drive or rotary punch

Decorative pattern tools (page 18)

Painting and dyeing supplies (pages 19-21)

Stitching needs (page 25)

A wonderful idea for a gift or just a unique piece of leather décor, a handmade catchall tray is a functional piece of art with endless uses.

For this project, we will use a thicker piece of leather so that the piece will hold its shape; 4–5 oz or 5–6 oz are ideal weights. You don't need a pattern to make this tray; all you need is a carpenter's square and your basic leatherworking tools.

TECHNIQUE REVIEW

▶ Branding Leather (pages 38–39)

▶ Carving Leather (pages 40–41)

▶ Adding Color (pages 42–47)

▶ Stitching (pages 57–60)

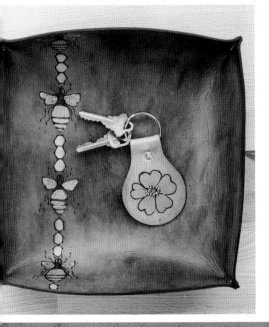

1 DETERMINE THE TRAY SIZE

A popular size is 8" (20.3cm) square by 1½" (3.8cm) tall; it fits keys, a wallet, a cell phone and a few other small things, but you can make yours as large or as small as you'd like. Small trays work well for jewelry, and you can make extra-large ones for the mail.

Choose your dimensions, including the depth of your tray. These trays are relatively shallow, so a depth between 1" (2.5cm) and 2½" (6.4cm) works best.

2 DRAW YOUR RECTANGLE AND CUT IT OUT

Determine the dimensions for your rectangle using these guidelines: To find the width of the rectangle, add the width you chose for the finished tray plus twice the depth of the finished tray. Similarly, the length of the rectangle is the length of the finished tray plus twice the depth. For example, if you are making an 8" × 5" × 1½" (20.3cm × 12.7cm × 3.8cm) tray, the width of the rectangle will be 8" (20.3cm) and the length will be 11" (27.9cm).

Thicker hides are more prone to imperfections on the back than lighter-weight leathers, so check your hide carefully for thin spots, nicks and other blemishes on the front and the back. It's much better to find these blemishes before you start your project. Use your carpenter's square to draw the rectangle onto your leather and cut it out.

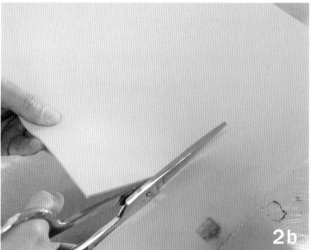

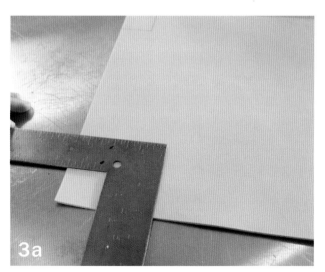

3 CUT THE CORNER SQUARES

Use your carpenter's square to mark squares on each corner of the rectangle using the depth of the tray as your side length of the square. For a tray 1½" (3.8) deep, draw 1½" (3.8cm) squares on the corners of the tray. Cut out the squares with a knife or sharp scissors.

4 MARK AND PUNCH YOUR STITCHING HOLES

Mark the stitch holes along the edges of the inverted corners. For a tray with a depth of 1½"–2" (3.8cm–5.1cm), five holes on each side of the inverted corner work best. The holes don't have to be perfectly spaced; just mark one at the middle, one at each end, and then two additional holes in between on each side. The holes should be about ⅛" (3mm) from the edge.

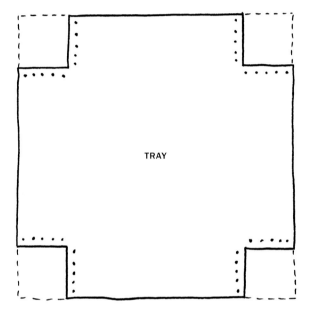

TRAY

FOR CONSISTENT SPACING

To keep your holes a consistent distance from the edge, set your drawing compass to ¼" (6mm) and place the non-marking end of the compass at the edge of the leather so the pencil is ¼" (6mm) from the edge. Drag your compass along the edge of the leather to make a line ¼" (6mm) in and parallel to the edge.

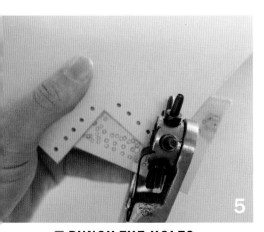

5 PUNCH THE HOLES

Punch the holes using a size 00 punch.

6 BRAND OR CARVE THE LEATHER

Sketch your design onto the leather. Decide if you want to carve or brand your design. Carving works very well because this leather is thick. Branding works well, too, as these trays won't see much wear or bending over their lifetime.

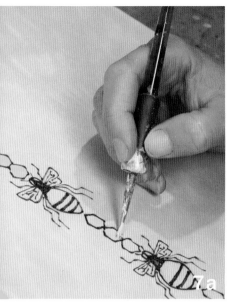

7 PAINT, DYE AND ADD THE TOPCOAT

Once your decorative pattern is applied, paint it, dye it and add a protective topcoat just as we did in earlier projects. Put the tray on a rack to dry.

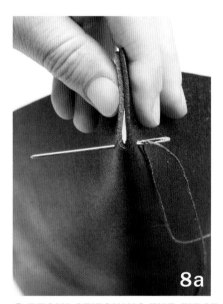
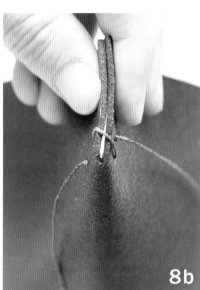

8 BEGIN STITCHING THE FIRST CORNER

Cut a piece of thread about 15" (38.1cm) long and thread a needle (blunt needles will work best). With the tray face up, pull up the sides of the tray so the corners align. Working on the back side of the tray (the flesh side of the leather) pull the thread halfway through the first set of holes. Then take one needle and cross the thread over to the next hole on the opposite side. Stitch through this set of holes, then take the other needle and do the same. When you get to the set of holes halfway up the edge, run one needle through the holes an extra time for added security.

9 FINISH STITCHING

Continue stitching, crossing over your stitches and alternating needles, until you get to the top holes. Secure your stitches at the top by running one of the needles through the top set of holes one to two times more.

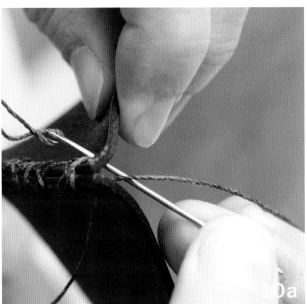

10 TIE OFF THE THREAD

When you reach the top set of holes, knot the thread together on the inside of the tray and trim the ends. Repeat steps 8–10 with the remaining three corners.

POUCH

MATERIALS

2-3 oz leather

Segma or Line 20 snap

Hand snap setter (and mallet) or press

If riveting edges: rivets (quantity varies), hand rivet setter (and mallet) or press

If stitching edges: stitching needs (page 25)

For optional wristlet or purse: D-ring and swivel snap (2 of each for purse), rivets, splitter and strap (½" [1.3cm], ⅝" [1.6cm] or ¾" [1.9cm] wide)

Cardstock and sharp paper scissors

Marking and cutting tools (pages 14-16)

Punching tools (page 17), including size 2 (⅛" [3.2mm]) and size 7 (⁷⁄₃₂" [5.6mm]) drive or rotary punch for Segma snap, size 6 (³⁄₁₆" [4.8mm]) for Line 20 snap and size 00 (¹⁄₁₆" [1.6mm]) if stitching or size 1 (³⁄₃₂" [2.4mm]) for rivets

Decorative pattern tools (page 18)

Painting and dyeing supplies (pages 19-21)

One of the earliest pieces I created was a little pouch. It was a simple design, just one piece of leather folded over twice with rivets at the sides and a snap closure. I still have the first pouch that I made, and I carried it in my purse for years. Now I carry no fewer than three or four. These little pouches make great organizers for a bag or can be used alone as a clutch.

Make your pouch any size you want; take a look at what you want to store in it and measure your little components. These pouches will start out relatively flat and develop dimension with time, so they work best for carrying items that are relatively flat themselves—no more than ½" (1.3cm) or so thick. Choose a lighter-weight leather for this project.

TECHNIQUE REVIEW

► Preparing and Tracing Your Pattern (page 32)

► Cutting Out Your Pattern (page 33)

► Branding Leather (pages 38–39)

► Adding Color (pages 42–47)

► Attaching Hardware (pages 50–53)

► Stitching (pages 57–60)

DOUBLE SNAP

If you're making a wider pouch like the ones shown here, add a second snap to help keep the flap shut. Remember, Line 20 snaps will be more prominent than Segma snaps.

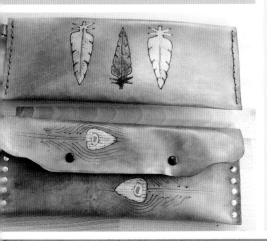

1 DETERMINE YOUR MEASUREMENTS

Measure the things that you would like to fit in the pouch to get approximate dimensions for the piece. Add about 1" (2.5cm) to the width to accommodate the rivets; this is the width for your pattern. If you want to use the pouch for something especially bulky, make the pouch slightly larger to accommodate.

The length of the pattern is going to be 2½ to 2¾ times the height measurement of the pouch. The exact calculation depends on how long you would like the flap to be.

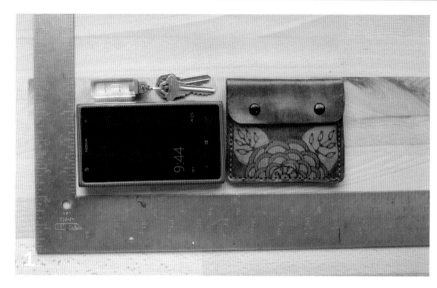

 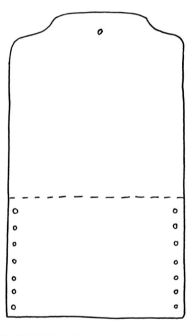 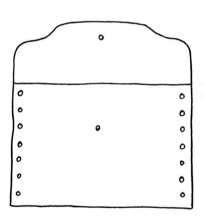

2 DRAW YOUR PATTERN SHAPE

Draw a rectangle on a piece of cardstock using the dimensions from step 1. Draw the shape of your flap on the top edge of the rectangle. You can leave it square, round the corners or make it curvy. Do remember that soft curves tend to wear better than hard corners, which blunt and lose their shape over time.

When you have shaped the flap, cut out your pattern piece. Mark a hole on the flap for the snap, about ½" (1.3cm) in from the bottom edge of the flap. Punch this hole.

3 START THE PATTERN HOLES

On the opposite end from the shaped flap, mark a line the height of your pouch in from the end of the pattern. This is the fold line on your finished piece.

Mark your line for rivets or stitching: Starting at the bottom of the pattern piece, draw a line on both sides up to the fold line, ¼" (6mm) from the edge for stitches, ⅜" (1cm) for rivets. Mark and punch your holes along these lines. The last hole should be no closer than ⅛" (3mm) from the fold line.

4 TRANSFER THE REMAINING HOLES

Fold your piece along the fold line and transfer your hole marks to what will become the back of your pouch. Punch the transferred hole marks.

Then, with the bottom portion of the pouch folded up, fold your flap down. Don't fold it tightly, but rather leave an ⅛" (3mm) of give. This allows the leather ample space to fold. Mark the hole for the snap on the body of the pouch and punch it.

5 CUT THE PATTERN OUT OF LEATHER

Lay the pattern on your piece of leather and trace around it. Cut the leather and punch the holes where indicated, using a size 00 punch for stitching holes and a size 1 punch for rivets. Punch the holes for the snap, using a size 6 punch for a Line 20 snap or a size 2 punch for the male side of a Segma snap and a size 7 punch for the female side.

6 ADD THE DESIGN AND BRAND

Draw your decorative pattern in pencil, then brand the design. Because the leather is thin for this project, carving will not work.

7 ADD PAINT, OIL, DYE AND TOPCOAT

Apply rubbing alcohol first, then paint your design. When the paint is dry, apply the oil. When the oil is dry, dye the piece. Let the dye dry, then add the topcoat. Let dry.

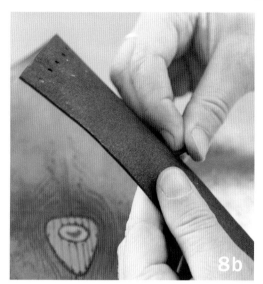
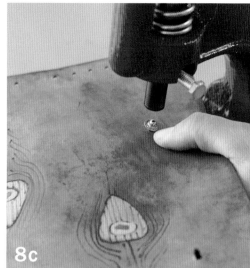

8a

8b

8c

8 ADD THE SNAP

To set the Segma snap, put the female connective piece through the flesh side of the flap. Put the cap over it and set with a press or with your hand snap setter tools. Put the post end of the male piece through the flesh side of the body of the piece, then put the connective side of the male piece on top of it on the grain side and set. (In the photos, I'm setting two snaps on the flap.)

To set the Line 20 snap, put the female post side through the grain side of the flap and then the connector portion on the post on the flesh side. Set with a press or your hand snap setter tools. Put the male post portion through the flesh side on the body of the bag, and then put the male connector portion on top of it on the grain side and set.

9 STITCH OR RIVET THE SIDES

If you are riveting, it is best to put all the rivets in at the same time and lock the caps before you set them. This helps to keep the entire pouch together and the holes properly aligned while you are setting the rivets. You can set them with hand tools or with a press.

If you are stitching, a running stitch or a modified blanket stitch both work well. You want something that is going to hold the edges together tightly, as this piece will see a lot of use.

10 CHECK THE FOLDS

Check the fold lines on the flap and bottom; touch up any cracks or areas that need more dye. Then you're done!

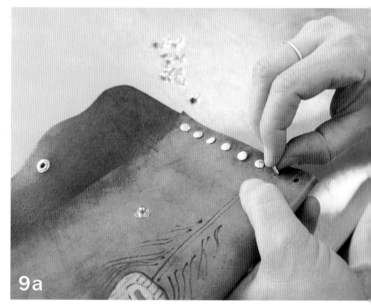

9a

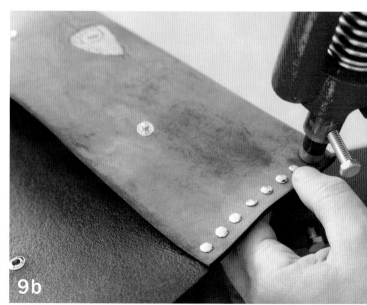

9b

ADDING A STRAP

Want to use this piece as a purse or a wristlet? No problem! You'll need some D-rings (one for a wristlet, two for a purse), swivel snaps (again, one for a wristlet, two for a purse) and some rivets.

To make a wristlet, cut a small leather tab, about 1½" × ½" (3.8cm × 1.3cm) and fold it in half around a small D-ring (dye the tab to match your piece first!). Place the ends between the layers of leather on one side of the pouch (near the opening) and punch holes in the tab where the stitching or rivet holes are (Figure 1). Stitch or rivet the tab to the side of the pouch, D-ring out, when you are assembling the pouch (Figure 2).

To make the wrist strap, cut a piece of strap leather ⅝" × 12" (1.6cm × 30.5cm). Split one end 2½" (6.4cm) in and the other end ½" (1.3cm) in (refer to step 3 of the Belt project). Fold the 2½" (6.4cm) split end over a swivel snap, leaving ½" (1.3cm) of the 2" (5.1cm) exposed. Rivet the swivel snap on. Fold the other end so it meets the riveted end. Rivet this end in place (Figure 3). Snap the strap onto the D-ring.

To make a purse, begin as you did for the wristlet, but add a second tab and D-ring to the other side of the pouch. Cut a shoulder strap ⅝" × 50" (1.6cm × 127cm) from leather. Split the ends 2" (5.1cm) in. Round the corners for a more finished look. Fold each end over a swivel snap and rivet them in place. Clip each strap end onto a D-ring.

FIGURE 1

FIGURE 2

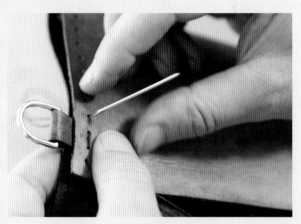

FIGURE 3

SMALL WALLET

MATERIALS

2-3 oz leather

For wallet back, if carving: 4-5 oz leather

For optional closure: 2 Segma snaps, hand snap setter (and mallet) or press

Cardstock and sharp paper scissors

Marking and cutting tools (pages 14-16)

Punching tools (page 17), including size 00 (1/16" [1.6mm]) drive or rotary punch for stitching, size 2 (1/8" [3.2mm]) and size 7 (7/32" [5.6mm]) drive or rotary punch for optional snaps

Decorative pattern tools (page 18)

Painting and dyeing supplies (pages 19-21)

Stitching needs (page 25)

Small, functional, and just as stylish as you want it to be, a leather wallet is something you will certainly use every day. We will start with a simple one. If you want to get more complicated, making additional pockets and the like, you will learn how to do this in the *Smartphone Case* project (page 110). For now, we'll create a simple wallet that will work beautifully for cash and a few credit cards, or some business cards.

TECHNIQUE REVIEW

- ▶ Preparing and Tracing Your Pattern (page 32)
- ▶ Cutting Out Your Pattern (page 33)
- ▶ Branding Leather (pages 38–39)
- ▶ Carving Leather (pages 40–41)
- ▶ Adding Color (pages 42–47)
- ▶ Attaching Hardware (pages 52–53)
- ▶ Stitching (pages 57–60)

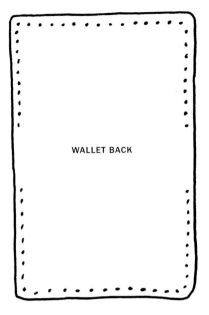

WALLET BACK

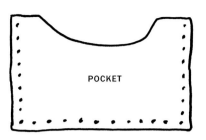

POCKET

1 MAKE THE PATTERN

This wallet requires two pattern pieces: the wallet back and the pocket. You will cut the pocket from your leather two or three times, depending on whether you would like a pocket on the back of the wallet as well.

For the pocket, draw a 4⅜" × 2⁵⁄₁₆" (11.1cm × 5.9cm) rectangle on your cardstock. The long sides are the top and bottom of the pocket; shape the top of the pocket so it is easier to access your cards. On the bottom, round the two bottom corners slightly, just enough to take the square edges off. Square edges get dinged and become rounded or folded over time, so starting out rounded, or at least not perfectly square, will result in a nicer look.

For the wallet back, draw a 4⅜" × 5⁵⁄₁₆" (11.1cm × 13.5cm) rectangle. Using the pocket pattern piece as a guide, round the corners of the wallet back.

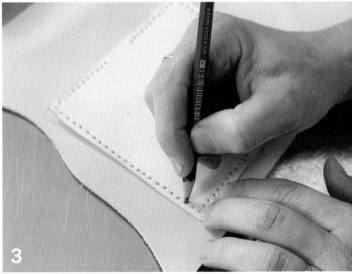

2 MARK YOUR HOLES

To mark the holes in the pocket, use your drawing compass or ruler to make a line ¼" (6mm) in from the edge on all sides except the top. Mark and punch holes on one half of the piece along the line, then fold the pocket in half and transfer the markings to the other half. Punch the holes with a size 00 punch.

Transfer the holes to the back piece of the wallet, aligning the pocket piece with the edges on each end of the back piece.

3 CUT THE PATTERNS FROM THE LEATHER

Lay your pattern pieces on the leather and trace them. If you want a third pocket on the outside of the wallet, trace your pocket piece three times. I like to make the top of the third pocket straight. Transfer your hole marks, then cut out and punch (with a size 00 punch) your pieces.

4 BRAND OR CARVE YOUR DESIGN

If you went with a 4–5oz piece of leather for the wallet back, the leather is thick enough to carve your design. You may brand the leather as well.

5 ADD PAINT, OIL, DYE AND TOPCOAT

Apply rubbing alcohol to the leather before painting your design to help the paint adhere. Once the paint is dry, oil all of the pieces, then apply the dye. When the dye is dry, add the topcoat. Place all pieces on a drying rack to dry.

6 ASSEMBLE THE WALLET

Cut a piece of thread approximately 2½ times the distance you need to stitch. A running stitch will work best for this, or a modified blanket stitch would work as well. Place the first pocket against the inside of the back piece, grain sides together. Beginning at the corner, pull your thread halfway through and stitch all the way around once, locking your stitches at the end. Thread your needle through the remaining thread and stitch around the wallet in the opposite direction, again locking your stitches at the end.

Lay the second pocket on the back inside piece, grain sides together, the mirror image of the first pocket. If you're including a third, outside pocket, place it so that the flesh side of the pocket is against the grain side of the wallet, aligning the holes of the inside pocket, the wallet back and the outside pocket. Stitch through all three pieces just as you did with the first pocket.

Check the folded areas and edges for any spots that need touching up. Then you're done.

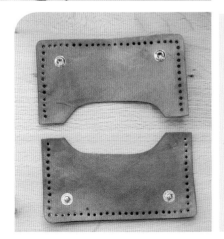

KEEP IT CLOSED

Want a wallet that stays closed? Mark and punch two snap holes with a size 7 punch on the bottom corners of the inside pockets, each ½" (1.3cm) in from either edge (use your carpenter's square to do this). Before you stitch the wallet, put a set of male snaps in one pocket and a set of female snaps in the other (using the Segma snaps). The connective pieces should be visible on the grain side of the piece so when you close it, they snap together.

TABLET CASE

MATERIALS

3-4 oz leather

Silicone or TPU case to fit your tablet

Line 20 snap

Hand snap setter (and mallet) or press

Cardstock and sharp paper scissors

Marking and cutting tools (pages 14-16)

Punching tools (page 17), including size 00 (1/16" [1.6mm]) drive or rotary punch for stitching, size 6 (3/16" [4.8mm]) for snap and punch size to match your tablet's camera hole (or hand-cut with craft knife)

Decorative pattern tools (page 18)

Painting and dyeing supplies (pages 19-21)

Stitching needs (page 25)

When tablets first came out, leather cases to hold them weren't far behind. The cases work fine, but over time the chromium-tanned leather wears through since it is thin, the stiffeners break down and the machine stitching falls apart. I wanted to create a leather cover that wouldn't stretch or warp. The pattern I came up with involves stitching a premade silicone case inside a leather cover. The silicone case holds the tablet securely, and the leather cover provides protection and style.

If you can find a silicone or TPU (thermoplastic polyurethane) inner case for your tablet, you can make yourself a beautiful outer case that doesn't require removing the tablet to use it. For this project you will be constructing your own pattern, since the dimensions of each tablet are different. I recommend a 3–4 oz leather; it will be thin enough to easily fold at the spine, but still thick enough to give the case some rigidity and protect your tablet.

TECHNIQUE REVIEW

- ▶ Preparing and Tracing Your Pattern (page 32)
- ▶ Cutting Out Your Pattern (page 33)
- ▶ Branding Leather (pages 38–39)
- ▶ Carving Leather (pages 40–41)
- ▶ Adding Color (pages 42–47)
- ▶ Attaching Hardware (pages 52–53)
- ▶ Stitching (pages 57–60)

OUTSIDE COVER

INSIDE COVER

TAB

1 MAKE THE PATTERN

Your pattern is comprised of three pieces: an outer cover that wraps all the way around the tablet, two inside covers (cut from the same pattern piece), and one closure tab.

Measure the length, width and height of your silicone case. To create the inside cover pattern piece, draw a rectangle on cardstock that is 1" (2.5cm) larger in length and width than your silicone case. This gives you a ½" (1.3cm) margin for stitching. Round the corners on one long side.

For the outside cover pattern, draw a rectangle the same height as the inside cover piece and twice the length of your inside cover plus twice the thickness of your silicone insert (this is essentially the spine measurement for your case). Round the corners. For the closure tab, draw a rectangle 3½" × 1" (8.9cm × 2.5cm). Round one end of the tab.

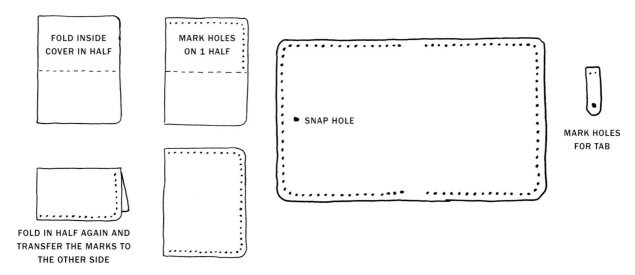

FOLD INSIDE COVER IN HALF

MARK HOLES ON 1 HALF

FOLD IN HALF AGAIN AND TRANSFER THE MARKS TO THE OTHER SIDE

SNAP HOLE

MARK HOLES FOR TAB

2 ADD THE STITCHING HOLES

To create a symmetrical pattern, take your inside cover piece and fold it in half from top to bottom. Open it up, mark and punch your holes on one half (using a size 00 punch), then refold and transfer your holes to the other half. Mark and punch the holes. Then, align this piece to each end of your back piece and mark the holes. Because the piece is symmetrical, you won't have to worry about keeping right sides together, or which side is up.

To mark the holes for the tab, choose which portion will be the cover front of the outer cover piece and mark a hole 1" (2.5cm) in from the edge centered along the long edge of the front. Then mark a centered hole ½" (1.3cm) from the rounded end of the tab for the snap. On the other end of the tab, transfer the holes from the center of the back of outer cover piece (you'll sew the tab in place along this edge). The holes should be approximately ½" (1.3cm) from the straight end.

3 CUT OUT THE LEATHER
Trace your patterns to your leather, cut out the pieces and punch them (stitching holes with a size 00 punch, snap holes with a size 6).

4 ADD THE DECORATIVE PATTERN, PAINT, DYE AND TOPCOAT
You can put pattern anywhere and everywhere you like; just remember that the back inside piece will be covered with the silicone insert. Brand (and/or lightly carve) your design, then apply rubbing alcohol, paint, oil, dye and topcoat, drying between coats. Move your decorated pieces to a drying rack and let them dry completely.

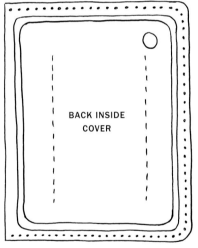

5 ADD THE SNAP
Using a Line 20 snap, set the male portion to the large back piece of your tablet case and the female to the small tab.

6 MARK HOLES FOR THE CASE
Mark two lines of holes in the back inside cover piece, approximately 1¼" (3.2cm) in from each side; if you are using a hard TPU case, mark and punch the holes in the case first, then transfer them to the leather. The exact location of the holes will depend on your tablet; make sure the stitches don't interfere with the camera (you will cut out a hole for the camera, if you have one, later). The stitching should be set just slightly in from the edges of the tablet.

Once you have marked the holes, punch them with a size 00 punch. Remember, if you're using a hard rubber TPU case, punch the holes in the case first. If you're using silicone, mark and punch the holes on the leather only; the needle will go through the silicone without punching it first.

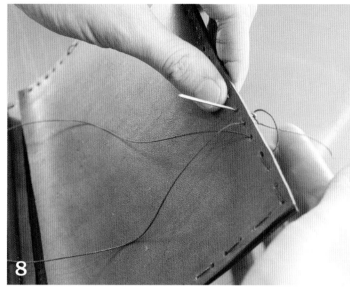

7 STITCH THE CASE TO THE BACK INSIDE COVER

Securely stitch your case to the punched leather piece. Tie knots in the thread or lock your stitches. I usually tie a knot on the inside; it's less likely to come undone with wear.

8 STITCH THE INSIDE COVER PIECES IN PLACE

Align the holes the on front inside cover piece with the outside cover, flesh sides together. Stitch the pieces together. Do the same for the back inside cover piece (with the case attached). When you get near the center, slide the tab between the layers of leather and stitch it in place.

A running stitch or cobbler's stitch works best for this type of piece (a cobbler's stitch is just like a running stitch, but you use two needles on opposite ends of the thread, going in the same direction at the same time). Or use a modified blanket stitch, wrapping your stitches around the side of the piece as well.

9 MAKE THE CAMERA HOLE

If you have a camera hole in the back of your case, the final step is to cut out the hole. If the hole is a circle and you have an appropriately sized drive punch, cut the hole with a drive punch. Otherwise, trace the outline of the hole onto the leather with your pencil. Carefully cut the hole out with a leather knife or craft knife.

After you cut out the hole, use a little dye and topcoat to touch up the leather where you cut.

DESIGN VARIATIONS

Want to mix it up? Instead of a tab closure, you can add a full flap that folds over, creating the closure. Add a twist-lock clasp to the flap, a magnetic closure or just a regular snap. When you draw your pattern, extend the width of the outside cover on the side that holds the tablet to create the flap. I find it useful to assemble the back of the piece first (stitch the silicone in place, then stitch the back inside cover with the silicone piece attached to the outer cover piece, centering it with the added flap to the right) and then place the other inside cover where it belongs but do not stitch. Punch a hole in the flap where you would like the snap or other closure, then fold it over as you would if you were closing it to

make the mark on the outside cover. Add both closures, then stitch the inside covers in place.

You can also use rivets on the edges instead of stitching them. When you create your pattern, mark your holes slightly further in from the edge, approximately ⅜" (1cm) instead of ¼" (6mm), and leave about ¼" (6mm) or more between the holes. You will still need to stitch the silicone insert into your tablet case, and you will also want to be careful when placing your tab closure, since you will need to have a rivet go through it. Use small rivets, preferably double-capped, since both sides of the rivet will be visible when your piece is finished.

JOURNAL COVER

MATERIALS

2-3 oz or 3-4 oz leather

For optional closure: Line 20 snap, hand snap setter (and mallet) or press

Cardstock and sharp paper scissors (optional)

Backing sheet (cardboard or thick piece of leather)

Leathercraft cement or adhesive

Marking and cutting tools (pages 14–16), including carpenter's square

Punching tools (page 17), including size 00 (⅟₁₆" [1.6mm]) drive or rotary punch for stitching and size 6 (³⁄₁₆" [4.8mm]) for optional snap

Decorative pattern tools (page 18)

Painting and dyeing supplies (pages 19-21)

Stitching needs (page 25)

Journal or book to cover

People often ask if I make the books that I sell, but I'm a leatherworker, not a bookbinder. There is barely enough space in my studio for all of my leather stuff, let alone stacks of paper. If you find yourself in a similar predicament, a prebound blank book makes a wonderful thing to cover with a bit of leather art. The bonus here is that this technique will work with any type of book: photo album, scrapbook, day planner, journal. I prefer leather on the thin side for this; 2–3 oz will fit tightly around the book. You can go slightly thicker, 3–4 oz, if you prefer; this will create a more rigid cover and add more bulk. Choose your favorite book, blank or otherwise, and let's make a cover for it.

TECHNIQUE REVIEW

▶ Preparing and Tracing Your Pattern (page 32)

▶ Cutting Out Your Pattern (page 33)

▶ Branding Leather (pages 38–39)

▶ Carving Leather (pages 40–41)

▶ Adding Color (pages 42–47)

▶ Attaching Hardware (pages 52–53)

▶ Stitching (pages 57–60)

1 MEASURE YOUR BOOK

Choose what you want to cover, then measure it with a cloth tape measure. Measure the distance around the book—from the edge of the back cover, around the spine, to the edge of the front cover while the book is closed—as well as the width of the front cover, the width of the spine and the height of the book. Write down these measurements.

2 DETERMINE THE COVER MEASUREMENTS

The cover is made of an outer cover, two smaller inside cover pieces (these hold the book in place) and an optional closure tab. For the outer cover, add 1" (2.5cm) to the total distance around the book and the height measurement. Adding an inch (2.5cm) to the length and width allows space for your stitching allowance.

The two inside cover pieces are the same height as the outer piece, and 1"–2" (2.5cm–5.1cm) narrower than the width of the front cover measurement you took in step 1. Don't try to make the inside covers as wide as the bound cover; leaving too narrow an opening in your book jacket will make it impossible to get the book in and out (trust me).

The tab closure should measure about 1" (2.5cm) wide. For the length, add 2" (5.1cm) to the width of the book spine. Round one end of the tab.

3 CUT THE LEATHER

You can transfer these measurements directly to your leather using a carpenter's square if you'd like to skip the pattern-making step. However, if you plan on making multiple covers, I recommend making a pattern the first time; it will save you time on your next cover.

PUNCH NOW, OR LATER?

The construction of this cover varies slightly from previous projects: The holes are punched after the leather has been decorated. If the idea of punching holes in your finished piece is too terrifying, stop here and punch the holes now. Begin with the holes in the inside cover, then place the punched inside cover on top of the unpunched inside cover, both with right sides up. Transfer the holes with your pencil and punch with a size 00 punch.

To add the holes to the outer piece, take one of the inside pieces and, right sides together, transfer the holes to the front and to the back of the piece. You will have to rotate it between marking the front and back to get the alignment correct.

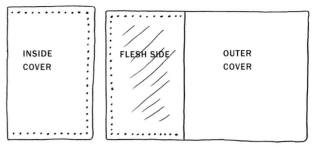

TRANSFER HOLES (FIRST SET)

ROTATE AND TRANSFER HOLES (SECOND SET)

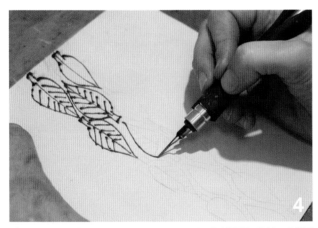

4 ADD DECORATIVE PATTERN, PAINT, OIL, DYE AND TOPCOAT

If you decided to use a 3–4 oz leather, you can carve it lightly. Otherwise it is best suited for branding and/or painting. Once you have put on your decorative pattern, oil it, dye it, topcoat it and let it dry.

5 ADD THE SNAP

If you are putting a snap closure on your book, make a mark 1" (2.5cm) in from the center front of your cover. Punch a hole with a size 6 punch there. Make a second hole in the center of the rounded end of your tab. Using a Line 20 snap, set the female snap into the tab and the male snap into the body of the book cover.

6a

6b

6 APPLY THE GLUE

Make a light pencil mark on the inside of the outer cover where it overlaps with the inside cover pieces so you know how far to glue. Using either Barge or other leathercraft cement (I used EcoWeld), make a thin line of glue around the inside edge of the outer cover, being careful to glue only about ¼" (6mm) to ⅜" (1cm) from the edge. Remember that you left only ½" (1.3cm) on either side for a stitching allowance, so your stitches should be no more than ⅜" (1cm) from the edge.

Apply glue to the inside cover flaps in the same manner, but be careful to leave one long edge on each piece unglued: This edge is left open to slide in your book flap. Apply glue to the non-snap end of the tab on both the front and back so when you sandwich it between the outer and inner covers, it stays in place.

When you are gluing, apply a thin coat, but a coat nonetheless. There should be no globs (too heavy) or dry spots (too light). After you have applied the glue, allow it to dry to a light tack.

7a

7 STICK THE PIECES TOGETHER

When the glue has dried to a light tack, align the inside front of the journal cover with the inside of the back; press both pieces together.

For the back cover, I like to have the book in hand, sometimes even in the jacket, to get the snap distance correct. Snap the tab on, then with the book placed inside the leather cover, curve it around the book and put the other end between the back inside and outside covers. Unsnap the tab, keeping the glued end in place. Adjust the tab as needed, then stack the back inside cover piece on top, aligning the edges with the outside cover piece. Press the pieces together to make the glue stick.

7b

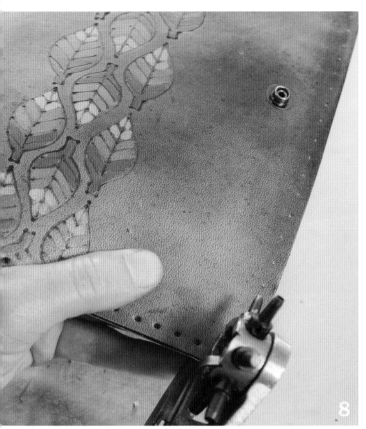

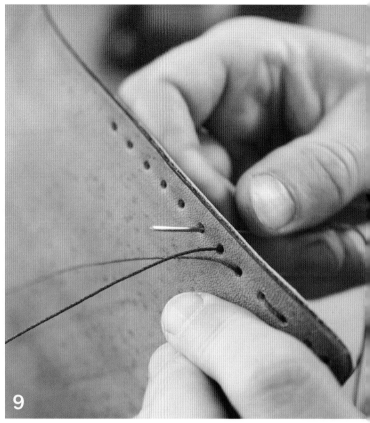

8 PUNCH THE HOLES

It can be a little nerve wracking to punch holes in a piece that you just spent all of this time crafting, but if you go slowly you'll be fine.

You can mark a very light line about ¼" (6mm) in from the edge of your piece to help with placement of the holes, but if you don't stitch completely over it, the line will be impossible to erase. You can also make a pattern template and mark the holes individually with a pencil. I usually just eyeball it. Your first hole should be approximately ⅛" (3mm) to ¼" (6mm) in from the end of the overlap of the inside and outside cover.

Punch your holes through the front of the leather with a size 00 punch and a backing sheet (piece of cardboard or a thick piece of leather) behind the piece to help the exit holes look cleaner.

Once you have put the holes in the front, repeat on the back. Make sure you have two holes (at least) in the tab to hold it in place securely.

If you prefer to have stitching all the way around the cover, you can add holes even where you are not stitching the two pieces of leather together. When your journal or book is closed, this will give the illusion of being entirely leather-bound. Otherwise, you'll have stitching only where necessary on the front and back.

9 STITCH THE PIECES

Use a running stitch or a modified blanket stitch to sew the pieces together. When your stitching is done, it's time for your book to try on its new jacket.

SAFETY REMINDER

Remember to work in a well-ventilated space when using leathercraft adhesive of any kind. Barge should be used outdoors when possible. Wear a respirator for extra protection.

SMARTPHONE CASE

MATERIALS

2–3 oz leather

For case back, if carving: 4–5 oz leather

Silicone phone case insert

Line 20 snap

Hand snap setter (and mallet) or press

Cardstock and sharp paper scissors

Leathercraft cement or adhesive (optional)

Marking and cutting tools (pages 14–16)

Punching tools (page 17), including size 00 (1/16" [1.6mm]) drive or rotary punch for stitching and size 6 (3/16" [4.8mm]) for snap

Decorative pattern tools (page 18)

Painting and dyeing supplies (pages 19–21)

Stitching needs (page 25)

I learned my lesson the hard way about why I should always, always, always keep my phone in a case. On a trip to the grocery store with my daughter I tried to put it back in my pocket, but instead the phone slipped out of my hand and onto the floor. It hit the very corner of the phone, just hard enough to crack the screen. When I got home the first thing my husband said to me was, "See, this is why you need to keep your phone in a case."

So, let's make our phones some little leather cases, shall we? The case is constructed very similarly to the tablet case we made earlier but has the option of adding a few pockets so you can keep cards in it as well. Leather that is 2–3 oz works well for the pockets. Go a little heaver (4–5 oz) for the phone case back if you'd like to carve your design. Next time you drop your phone (because it *will* happen), it will not shatter like mine did!

TECHNIQUE REVIEW

▶ Preparing and Tracing Your Pattern (page 32)

▶ Cutting Out Your Pattern (page 33)

▶ Branding Leather (pages 38–39)

▶ Carving Leather (pages 40–41)

▶ Adding Color (pages 42–47)

▶ Attaching Hardware (pages 52–53)

▶ Stitching (pages 57–60)

1 MAKE THE PATTERN

Just as you did for the tablet case, you will be constructing two inside covers for this case (one you will stitch the silicone to, and one for the inside front cover that you can put pockets on), an outer cover and a tab.

Measure the length and width of your silicone insert. Add ½" (1.3cm) to each of these dimensions to get the dimensions for the inside covers. The outside cover measures the same height as the inside cover; the width is twice the width of the inside cover plus twice the thickness of your phone. The tab closure can be relatively short: 2" × 1" (5.1cm × 2.5cm) should work for most phones. Draw your pattern pieces onto cardstock and cut them out, but do not mark holes on any of your pieces quite yet.

The pocket pieces (or credit card slots) will be 2½" (6.4cm) tall and the same width as the case inside cover.

Draw and cut one card slot; because they are a bit shorter than actual credit cards, you can leave the top straight or cut a small dip in the top. Mark one side of this pattern "UP." Take your inside cover pattern piece and mark 1 side "UP."

PUNCH NOW, OR LATER?

Your best bet for getting the hole alignment correct with your pieces is either to make a pattern and mark all of your holes on the pattern, or to skip punching and marking holes on your pieces at this point, and glue and punch them all at the end. The instructions on pattern making include how to correctly mark the holes on your pattern, but if you would prefer to glue and punch at the end, skip these instructions.

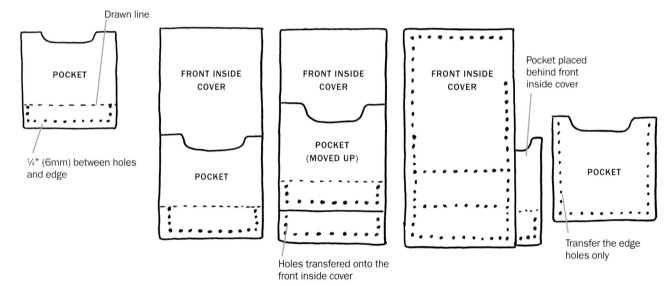

Drawn line

POCKET

¼" (6mm) between holes and edge

FRONT INSIDE COVER

POCKET

FRONT INSIDE COVER

POCKET (MOVED UP)

Holes transferred onto the front inside cover

FRONT INSIDE COVER

Pocket placed behind front inside cover

Transfer the edge holes only

POCKET

2 ADD HOLES TO THE PATTERN (IF PUNCHING NOW)

Decide how far apart you would like your card slots (I find that about ½" [1.3cm] works best) and make a line that far up on the pocket. Mark a line for holes ¼" (6mm) from the bottom and the sides up to your drawn line with the last hole on each side being placed on the drawn line, then mark and punch your holes.

Align your pocket piece with the bottom of your inside cover and transfer these holes to it. Move the pocket piece up, aligning the bottom holes on the pocket with the top holes that you just drew for the first pocket and transfer the holes again. Repeat once more to create a third pocket (the bottom of the highest pocket should be no less than 3¾" [9.5cm] from the top of the case).

Continue marking holes around the outside of your inside piece, ¼" [6mm] from the edge. You can leave the top right corner free of holes or continue marking the perimeter. Punch all of these holes with a size 00 punch. Place the pocket behind your inside piece, aligning the bottom holes. Transfer the edge holes only to the pocket pattern and punch them (do not mark and punch the holes that are in the center of the inside piece).

On the back inside piece, mark holes ¼" (6mm) from the edge along one long and two short sides. Mark holes 1" (2.5cm) in from the inside edge (the edge without holes), starting and stopping 1½" (3.8cm) from the top and bottom. Mark a second line of holes 1" (2.5cm) in from the outside edge (the edge with holes). Start 1" (2.5cm) from the bottom and stop, leaving enough space at the top to

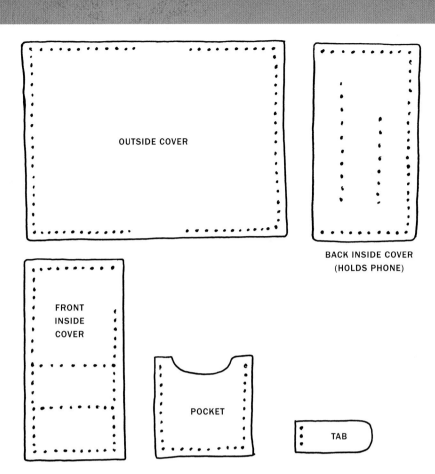

OUTSIDE COVER

BACK INSIDE COVER
(HOLDS PHONE)

FRONT
INSIDE
COVER

POCKET

TAB

accomodate a cutout for a camera, if your phone has one. Punch the holes with a size 00 punch.

Take the outside cover piece that you have cut and mark one side "FRONT" and "UP." On the front, place your front inside cover facedown with the holes for the pocket toward the bottom (assuming the front of your case is on the right and the back is on the left). Mark the edge holes only; do not mark the inside holes or any holes that fall in the center of the cover.

Place the back inside cover facedown on the opposite side of the outside cover piece. Mark the perimeter holes, then punch the holes with a size 00 punch.

Place your tab on the center back with just enough overlap to mark the holes. Mark the holes from the center back on the tab and punch.

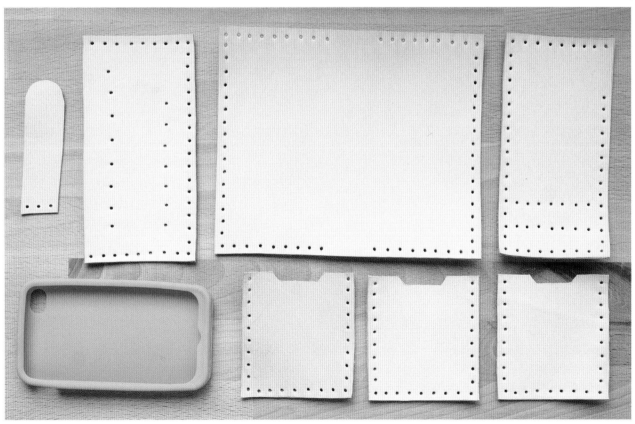

Completed pattern pieces

3 CUT THE PIECES FROM LEATHER

Trace the pattern pieces onto the leather Make sure that "UP" is visible when you are tracing them to the grain side of the leather. Unless you have taken steps to ensure symmetry (this would have been done when marking holes in the pocket), do not assume that your pieces are symmetrical. Cut three pockets, one back cover piece, one tab, and two inside pieces.

Transfer the holes you marked in the pattern pieces and punch them.

4 ADD DECORATIVE PATTERN

Add decorative pattern to your cover as desired. You can add pattern inside as well as outside, just remember that you will not see the part behind the phone. Brand and/or carve (if the outside cover is a heavier leather), add paint, dye, and topcoat and let dry.

4

CLOSURE ALTERNATIVE

If you would prefer a Velcro closure, skip step 5 and, after you have assembled your piece, use a sticky back hook-and-loop fastener dot on the body and on the tab. I've had good luck with these in temperate climates, but in warmer places the glue can come loose and the dot comes off.

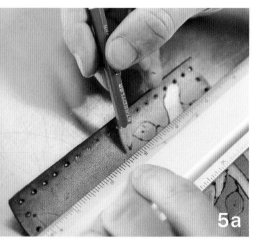

5a

5b

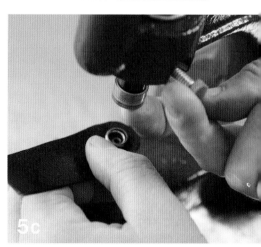

5c

5 ADD HARDWARE

This piece uses a snap closure. Mark a hole in the center of the rounded end of your tab. Also mark a hole ¾" (1.9cm) to 1" (2.5cm) from the outer edge of the cover, centered. Punch both holes with a size 6 punch and add a Line 20 snap. Put the female portion of the snap on the tab.

6 ATTACH THE PHONE INSERT

If you are using a TPU silicone insert, place the back inside cover facedown on the back of the insert, then mark and punch the holes in the insert. Stitch the case in place. For a soft silicone insert, do not prepunch holes in the insert; simply use a sharp needle to sew the case directly to the leather (the needle will pierce the insert).

Stitch the inside piece (with case attached) to the back of the cover (wrong/flesh sides together). Place the tab between the layers of leather with the flesh side toward the inside so it gets stitched in place.

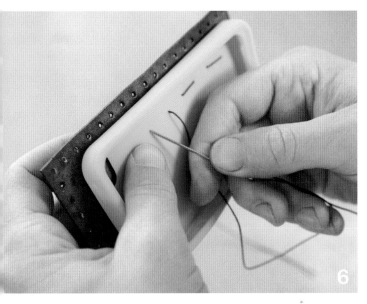

7 STITCH THE POCKETS

Starting with the right-hand side of the bottom pocket, stitch up along the side of the pocket until you reach the second pocket starting line. Place the second pocket behind the first, and stitch over and back on the bottom. Then stitch up along the side to the next pocket and stitch over and back along the bottom line for that pocket. Repeat for the third and final pocket.

Then continue your stitches up the right-hand side of the pocket inside piece until you reach the top. Reverse your stitch and stitch down to the bottom. When you reach the bottom hole, align this piece with the front of the cover piece and stitch them together starting with the bottom line of the bottom pocket.

> ### DON'T FORGET
> ·····································
> Be sure to lock your stitches at the beginning and end!

8 CUT THE CAMERA HOLE

Very carefully trace the camera hole onto the leather through the silicone insert. Using your knife, cut the hole. It may be helpful to punch a few holes with your drive punch to get started (or, if you happen to have a drive punch the size of the hole you need, use that). After the hole is cut, use a little bit of dye and topcoat to touch it up. You're done!

MESSENGER BAG

MATERIALS

4–5 oz or 5–6 oz leather for a structured bag, or 3–4 oz for a more relaxed look

For fixed-length strap: 1 leather strap, Line 24 snaps or swivel snap, hand snap setter (and mallet) or press

For adjustable strap: 1 leather strap, center-bar buckle, same width as strap, Line 24 snaps or swivel snap, hand snap setter (and mallet) or press

2 D-rings

Twist-lock clasp

Rivets

Hand rivet setter (and mallet) or press

Pliers

Cardstock and sharp paper scissors (optional)

Marking and cutting tools (pages 14–16), including carpenter's square and splitter

Punching tools (page 17), including size 1 (3⁄32" [2.4mm]) drive or rotary punch for rivets, size 00 (1⁄16" [1.6mm]) if stitching and size 6 (3⁄16" [4.8mm]) for optional snaps; also (for adjustable strap only) punch sized for holes that fit your buckle tongue, and end punch (optional)

Decorative pattern tools (page 18)

Painting and dyeing supplies (pages 20–21)

If stitching edges: stitching needs (page 25)

A messenger bag is something that you can, and will, use every day. It's also the biggest canvas that we have worked with yet, and it will give you plenty of space to cover with artwork.

A thinner leather (3–4oz) will get floppy over time and get that worn-in glove sort of look. Heavier leather, 4–5oz or 5–6oz, will hold shape over time but will add more weight to the bag. Choose the leather that works best for your purpose.

TECHNIQUE REVIEW

- ▶ Preparing and Tracing Your Pattern (page 32)
- ▶ Cutting Out Your Pattern (page 33)
- ▶ Branding Leather (pages 38–39)
- ▶ Carving Leather (pages 40–41)
- ▶ Adding Color (pages 42–47)
- ▶ Attaching Hardware (pages 50–56)
- ▶ Stitching (pages 57–60)

1 DETERMINE THE SIZE

What do you plan to carry in your bag: a laptop? A sketchbook? Both? Or maybe just a few small things, like a tablet, your wallet and cell phone. You can make the bag as big or as small as you like.

The dimensions of your messenger bag must be wider than the pieces you wish to carry in it. The construction of this bag has slightly tucked-in sides, so the outside width of the finished bag is wider than the inside dimension.

Once you know how wide you would like to make it, you need to decide if you want to rivet or stitch the edges. If you are riveting the edges, you need to add more space to allow for the rivets than if you are stitching.

DRAW A PATTERN OR MARK DIRECTLY

In step 2, you can make a pattern first and transfer it to the leather, or just draw your pieces directly onto the leather itself. Do whatever is easier for you. I prefer to draw directly on the leather.

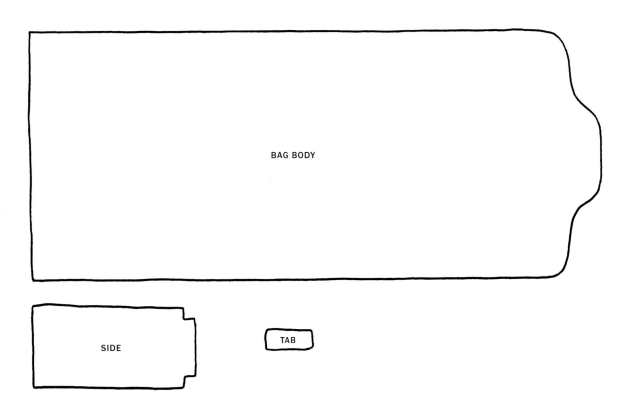

2 MAKE THE PATTERN ON CARDSTOCK

Using the dimensions you decided in step 1, add ½" (1.3cm) to the width if you are stitching and 1" (2.5cm) to the width if you are riveting. This is the width of your bag. To determine the length of the pattern piece, mutiply 2½ times the desired height of your bag plus 2 times the desired depth. Draw a rectangle with these dimensions for the body of your bag. Make the rectangle slightly longer if you would like a longer flap (as it is, your flap will be half the length of the bag).

Next, create two side pieces. For riveted sides, the width is the desired depth plus 1" (2.5cm) by your desired height plus ½" (1.3cm). For stitched sides, the width is the desired depth plus ½" (1.3cm) by your desired height plus ¼" (6mm). Cut a small square out of each of the bottom corners of your side pieces. These squares are the same size as your seam/rivet allowance: for a riveted bag, ½" (1.3cm) square and for a stitched bag, ¼" (6mm) square.

If you plan to add a strap to the bag, you need to make two small pieces to attach a D-ring to the bag; these will hold the strap on. The D-ring should be at least ½" (1.3cm) narrower than the side of your bag (not including the seam allowance). The tabs to attach it should be the same width as the D-ring and can be as long as you would like: This is an aesthetic judgment; they only need to be long enough to fold over the D-ring and be stitched or riveted in place. NOTE: When you choose your D-ring, you are also choosing the width of your shoulder strap. Generally the strap is the same width as the D-ring, though if you prefer an extra-wide strap, you can taper it at the ends or use a swivel snap to clip on the strap.

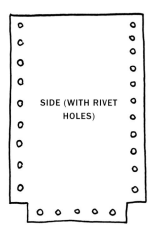

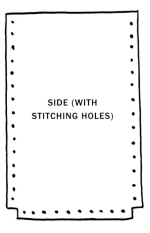

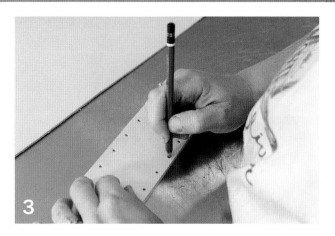

3 CUT OUT THE LEATHER AND MARK THE HOLES FOR THE SIDES

Transfer your pattern pieces (if made) to the leather and cut them out. Take one side piece and mark a line in the center of the seam or rivet allowance. Mark and punch your holes, being sure to stop at least ⅛" (3mm) from the edge for stitches and ¼" (6mm) from the edge for rivets. You can put the rivets as close together as your rivet caps will allow, but to hold the bag together you don't need any more than one every inch (2.5cm).

Once you have marked and punched your holes on one of the side pieces, transfer the same holes to the other side. It's best to do this with both pieces right side up, and the one with the holes on top; that way your sides are identical and if you mix them up, it isn't a problem. There is nothing more frustrating than having different right and left pieces and finding that you have riveted the left side piece to the right side of the bag.

CHOOSING RIVETS

To determine the proper size rivet for your bag, take two pieces of scrap from the leather that you are using and punch a hole. Try putting a small rivet through the hole. Does the end stick out just above the leather? Can you get the cap on? If you can get the cap on and it stays secure, the rivet is the right size. If you cannot put the cap on or see the end of the post through the leather, try the next size up. If you see the post of the rivet with both caps on, it is too long and you should try the next size down.

4 MARK HOLES FOR THE TABS

To determine the placement of the holes, fold the tab over the D-ring and make a light mark in the center of the tab ¼" (6mm) or more from the edge of the D-ring. This will leave sufficient space for the rivet setter; if you set it too close to the D-ring, the metal from the ring will stop the setter from compressing the rivet completely. Alternatively, you can stitch the tab in place. If you would like more than one hole in the tab, mark a second hole (and a third, if you have space). Punch the holes.

Place the tab where you would like it on a bag side piece. I place my D-rings so they are just above center, about two-thirds up the side of the bag. Make sure the tab is centered, then mark the holes on the side piece and punch them. Transfer the holes from your tab to the other tab, again right sides up, with the piece you just punched on top, and from the punched side piece to the other side piece.

5 TRANSFER THE HOLES TO THE BAG AND PUNCH

Let's start with the left side of your bag: With the opening edge of your bag to your left, take a side piece and lay it along the side closest to you so the top of the side piece and the top of the bag body are aligned. Your bag body should be grain side up, and your side piece flesh side up. With the sides flush, mark the holes and make a small line on the body of the bag where the side ends.

Rotate the side 90 degrees so the bottom of the side aligns with the side of your bag body. Move it slightly so that edge of the side aligns with the mark you just made. Mark the holes, and then mark where the bottom of your side piece ends on the side of the bag. Rotate the side piece again so the other edge of the side piece is now aligned with the side of your bag. Move the side piece slightly so the bottom edge aligns with the mark you just made. Mark the remaining holes.

Repeat this process on the other side of the bag. When all the holes are marked, use your carpenter's square to check and make sure that the little tick marks at the ends of the sides are directly across from one another on the bag. If the marks are slightly off, it won't matter, but if they're more than ⅛" (3mm), you'll need to redraw your holes and try again. Before punching the holes, double-check the top line of the bag to be sure it is straight and the side pieces for symmetry. Punch the holes.

5a   5b

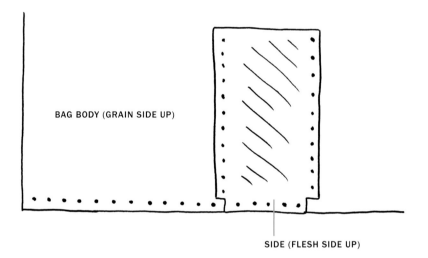

BAG BODY (GRAIN SIDE UP)

SIDE (FLESH SIDE UP)

EASY SYMMETRY

If you made a pattern for your bag (usually I don't because it's so big), mark the holes on your side piece and then mark the holes on one side of the bag body only. Fold the bag body in half and mark the same holes on the other side, making it symmetrical. The method described in step 5 will also work, but this method will give you more precise results.

ADJUSTABLE STRAP

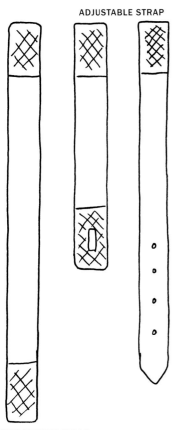

FIXED-LENGTH STRAP

 INDICATES SPLIT END

6a 6b

6 MAKE THE STRAP

Decide if you want an adjustable or fixed-length strap. For a fixed-length strap, cut the strap 3" (7.6cm) longer than the desired length; split about 3" (7.6cm) on each end of the strap (refer to step 3 of the Belt project). Punch a centered hole ½" (1.3cm) from one end of the strap and a second hole 2½" (6.4cm) from the end. Repeat on the other end of the strap. You can put either a rivet or snaps in these when you are assembling your bag.

For an adjustable strap, cut two pieces of leather. I like to make the piece that the buckle attaches to about 17" (43.2cm) long. For the buckle piece, split 3" (7.6cm) on each end. Cut a slot for the buckle in the center of one of the split ends. The other end will be for your snap or rivet. On the long strap piece, cut a tip at one end like you would on a belt (using an end punch if desired), and split 3" (7.6cm) on the other end.

FLAP SHAPE
. . . .

This is a good time to add some shape to your bag flap (the portion of your body piece without any holes in it). You can make it symmetrical, asymmetrical, whatever you'd like. Think about your pattern and what would look best with it, then cut the flap into your desired shape.

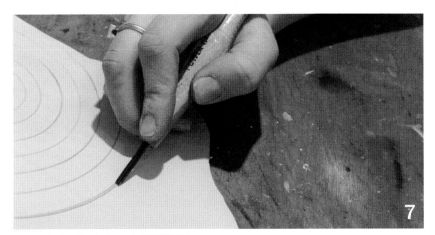

7

7 DECORATE THE LEATHER

We're using a heavier leather, so carving is a good choice for this piece. Remember that you don't have to limit your pattern to just the body of the bag; you can also decorate the sides, tabs and strap. Once you've added your pattern, remember to treat the leather with rubbing alcohol. Then add oil, dye and topcoat and let it dry.

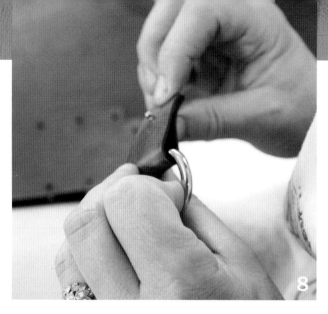

8 RIVET THE D-RINGS IN PLACE

It's important to do this first, because if you wait you won't be able to access that portion of your bag with your rivet setting tools very easily.

To attach the D-rings, thread a ring through one of your tabs and align the tab holes. Push a rivet through the tab holes and through the corresponding hole on the grain side of your bag. Set the rivet. Repeat with the other tab and side piece.

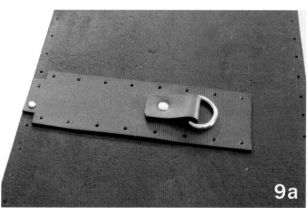

9a

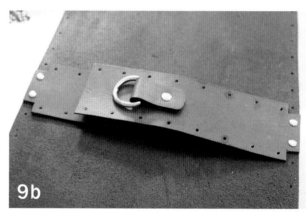

9b

9 ASSEMBLE THE SIDE AND BODY PIECES

If you are stitching your bag together, start on either side of the bag: Align the top of your side with the top of the bag, wrong sides together. Use a running stitch or modified blanket stitch to stitch all the way around and back on one side. Backstitch the first stitch to hold your thread in place. When you get to the corners, fold the bag sides up to make them square, just as you did with the sides of the *Catchall Tray* (see page 82). You can use your stitches to create more tension and give them a square shape, but it is helpful to work them with your hands as well.

If you are riveting, carefully count the holes on your side piece and bag, finding the corresponding bottom holes. Rivet the pieces together. Attach the bottom of the second side piece. Then rivet the sides together; this

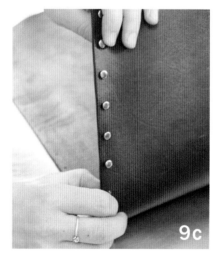

9c

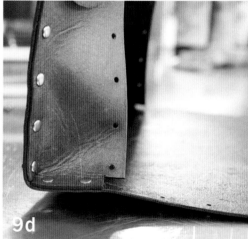

9d

makes it much easier to access those tricky holes in the corners of the bag. When you are riveting a side in place, be sure you have all of the rivets in the row in place before you begin to set them. Having all the rivets in will hold the alignment and ensure that all of the holes line up.

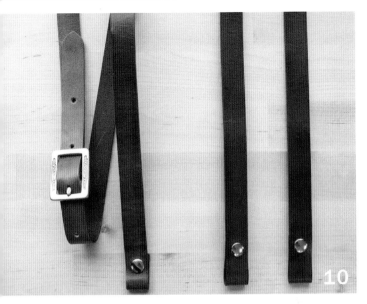

10 ADD THE STRAP

If you are making a fixed-length strap, you can use snaps at the end (Line 24 will work best; they are just like Line 20 but bigger), a swivel snap (just rivet it onto the end) or you can rivet the ends directly over the D-ring on your bag so the strap is permanent.

If you are making your strap adjustable, add a buckle to the short strap on the end that has a slot. Rivet the buckle in place. On the long strap, put adjustment holes on the end that you shaped; 2" (5.1cm) apart works well. The opposite ends on these straps can be attached to the bag in the same way you would attach the fixed-length strap, using snaps, swivel snaps or rivets.

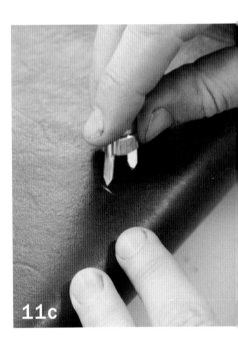

11 ADD THE CLOSURE

Once your bag is assembled, fold the flap over to the front of the bag and make sure it's the right length. If you think it is too long, and your decorative pattern doesn't need the extra length, trim the flap. Once you're happy with the flap length, decide where the closure will go. Center it well enough that it will keep the flap closed.

Using the oval portion of your twist-lock clasp, draw the oval where the closure will be on the flap of the bag. With a cutting mat (NOT YOUR BAG!) underneath it, carefully cut the oval with your craft or leather knife. Take the part of the twist-lock oval that has legs and push it through the front of the bag. Put the other oval piece on the back and bend the legs apart to keep it in place.

Next, take the turning portion of the twist-lock clasp and close your bag. Align the bag flap as you would when closed, and put the legs through the oval. Press to make two marks. Open your bag and carefully cut these 2 marks with your craft or leather knife, making cuts just large enough to slide the legs through. Slide the legs through the holes, and thread the backing piece on from the inside of your bag. Bend the legs toward each other with a pair of pliers. Take the flap of your bag and close it, turning the lock.

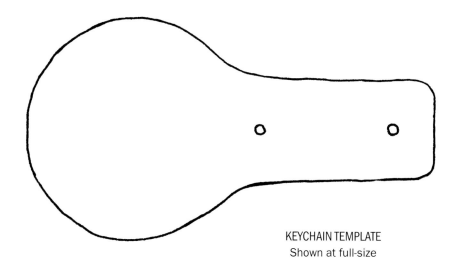

KEYCHAIN TEMPLATE
Shown at full-size

1" (2.5cm)
square

ABOUT THE AUTHOR

Caitlin McNamara Sullivan is the child of divorced parents who grew up split between households: one headed by two artists and the other by two writers. When she was young, her mother, a graphic designer, married a glass sculptor. Her father, a poet and English professor, married a poet and high-school English teacher. Caitlin, however, aimed at a career in law or math, earning bachelor's degrees in philosophy, mathematics and interdisciplinary visual arts while minoring in art history. She never imagined becoming an artist or writer herself.

Working with leather sparked a love that couldn't be denied. From 2004 through 2010, Caitlin worked full time as a paralegal in personal injury law and ran her leathercraft business at night and on weekends. In 2010, when her daughter was born, she left the law firm and turned to art fulltime. She is thankful every day that when she goes to work, she is doing something she enjoys.

Caitlin currently lives just north of her hometown of Seattle, Washington, with her husband, two kids, two dogs and two cats. Theirs is a house full of energy and life. When she's not at the studio making leather goods, Caitlin enjoys working in the yard and sewing small projects for the kids and their home. Creating and sharing her creations with the people in her life has always given her great joy. Caitlin hopes to pass a love of crafting on to her children as well as share it with her readers. Find more of her work at www.moxieandoliver.com.

DEDICATION

To my husband, who always believed the leather scraps I managed to spread to even the most remote corners of the house would turn into something wonderful.

And to all my loyal fans and customers who have supported Moxie & Oliver over the past ten years. Your belief in the value of handmade, and your love for my artwork, has changed my life. Without you, I would still be working at a law firm, and leathercraft would just be a hobby.

ACKNOWLEDGMENTS

Thank you to:

My dad and stepmother, for teaching me how to write.

My mom and stepdad, for teaching me how to create.

My husband, Kevin, again, since none of this would be possible without you.

Aife and Niall, my sweet, sweet children, for always having smiles for me to come home to.

Anna, Amy and Caitlin for testing out the projects and being my hand models.

Andy and Ian, for making sure I always have the supplies I need.

And Stephanie, my editor, for helping me put this all together into something cohesive.

Index

LeatherCrafted. Copyright © 2015 by Caitlin McNamar Sullivan. Manufactured in China. All rights reserved. It is permissible for the purchaser to create the designs contained herein and sell them at fairs, bazaars and craft shows. No other part of this book may be reproduced in any form or by any electronic or mechanical means including information storage and retrieval systems without permission in writing from the publisher, except by a reviewer who may quote brief passages in a review. Published by Fons & Porter Books, an imprint of F+W, A Content + eCommerce Company, 10151 Carver Road, Suite 200, Blue Ash, Ohio 45242. (800) 289-0963. First Edition.

a content + ecommerce company

www.fwmedia.com

19   18   17   16   15   5   4   3   2   1

DISTRIBUTED IN CANADA BY FRASER DIRECT
100 Armstrong Avenue
Georgetown, ON, Canada L7G 5S4
Tel: (905) 877-4411

DISTRIBUTED IN THE U.K. AND EUROPE BY F&W MEDIA INTERNATIONAL
Brunel House, Newton Abbot, Devon, TQ12 4PU, England
Tel: (+44) 1626 323200, Fax: (+44) 1626 323319
Email: enquiries@fwmedia.com

DISTRIBUTED IN AUSTRALIA BY CAPRICORN LINK
P.O. Box 704, S. Windsor NSW, 2756 Australia
Tel: (02) 4560 1600, Fax: (02) 4577 5288
E-mail: books@capricornlink.com.au

SRN: T2788
ISBN-13: 978-1-4402-4167-3

Edited by Stephanie White
Cover designed by Brianna Scharstein
Interior designed by Wendy Dunning
Production coordinated by Jennifer Bass
Photography and illustrations by Caitlin McNamara Sullivan

METRIC CONVERSION CHART

To convert	to	multiply by
Inches	Centimeters	2.54
Centimeters	Inches	0.4
Feet	Centimeters	30.5
Centimeters	Feet	0.03
Yards	Meters	0.9
Meters	Yards	1.1

Expand your crafting horizons
with these great books!

THESE AND OTHER FINE BOOKS ARE AVAILABLE AT YOUR LOCAL RETAILER AND ONLINE.

Visit **www.craftdaily.com** for tutorials, videos, lessons and workshops taught by world-class artists.